André Daigneault

THE LONG JOURNEY TOWARD SERENITY

To Recover Our Heart of a Child

Psychology and

Translated from:

LE LONG CHEMIN VERS LA SÉRÉNITÉ
Pour retrouver son coeur d'enfant

In the Arms of Mary Foundation
COMMUNION OF LIFE WITH CHRIST THROUGH MARY
Fort Collins, CO

Nihil Obstat: Reverend Father Joseph Son Thanh Nguyen, M.Div., M.A., S.T.D.
Censor Librorum

Imprimatur: +Most Reverend Kevin William Vann, J.C.D., D.D.
Bishop of Orange in California
USA – March 28, 2022

Previously printed in French as ***Le long chemin vers la sérénité***

870, Carré de Tracy Est, C.P. 7605
Charlesbourg, Québec
G1G 5W6, Canada

Published in English by:
In the Arms of Mary Foundation
P.O. Box 271987
Fort Collins, CO 80527-1987
E-mail address: inquiry@IntheArmsofMary.org
Website: www.IntheArmsofMary.org

Translated by
Andree M. Wagatha

Edited by
Mary Jane Bartee Joseph Winston Alcruz

Cover, text design and photo by
Ewa Krepsztul

"Decalogue for Faith Sharing" from Families of Nazareth Movement USA.

Used with permission.

In gratitude for Our Blessed Mother keeping us focused on Her Son.

ISBN 978-1-93-331467-9

CONTENTS

CHAPTER 10

APPENDIX

Let our reader understand that by citing, in passing, a certain novelist, philosopher, psychologist or sociologist, we do not mean to signify that we are necessarily in perfect agreement with the whole of his/her thinking. But like a Thomas Aquinas, who even remembered refuting erroneous doctrine to bring to light the truths it might contain, we always want to do justice to the truth. Because of this, from whatever perspective it comes, even be it from a non-Christian thinker, it remains the truth and always confirms these words of Jesus: "The truth will set you free."

The author

BIOGRAPHY OF ANDRÉ DAIGNEAULT

André Daigneault was born in Montréal in the working-class neighborhood of Saint-Henri. He spent his childhood and adolescence in Verdun and finished High School at the Richard school. Having a rather sickly childhood, he became an indefatigable reader: novels, poetry, psychology – everything interested him. He worked for a few years at Seagram while taking courses at Montréal University in poetry and literature, participated in a theater group, and published his first poems at the age of nineteen.

At the beginning of his twenties, he made a rediscovery of God which moved him deeply. It was then that he moved from Montréal to Québec City to engage with a group of lay people dedicated to the popular apostolate.

André Daigneault has had diversified commitments for most of his life. Early on, he was Editor-in-Chief at the magazine "Je Crois," a consecrated layman and priest since 1982, an animator for several years of La Rencontre Movement, a preacher and counselor, a talented poet and writer, and he has a rather special gift as a popularizer. After having been assistant-director and director-general of the secular

Institute Pius X, he now devotes himself mainly to the direction of retreats, as well as meetings with individuals, and to writing.

He is the author of several books, including two now translated into English by **In the Arms of Mary Foundation**: *The Way of Imperfection: Holiness for the Poor (Le chemin de l'imperfection: La sainteté des pauvres)* and this book, *The Long Journey toward Serenity: To Recover Our Heart of a Child (Le long chemin vers la sérénité: Pour retrouver son coeur d'enfant)*. Other titles popular in various international languages are *Du coeur de pierre au coeur de chair* [From a Heart of Stone to a Heart of Flesh], *Au coeur de la misère: la miséricorde* [In the Depth of Misery, Mercy], *La faiblesse transfigurée* [Mercy, Transfigured Weakness], all published by Les Éditions Le Renouveau, as well as several more works by other publishers.

Freud said that the poet sometimes manages to intuitively grasp in people what he himself took several years of analysis to discover. It is by this force of intuition, which characterizes André Daigneault so well, that this author manages to convey, in *The Long Journey toward Serenity*, the union between life and true faith, to lead us – beneath our shells – to peace of heart and serenity.

To have seen to be born and to die,
To love, to have been loved, to have been betrayed,
tortured by absences and lies:
To have cursed, to have forgiven,
to have forgotten the forgiveness,
and one day to envelop with the same friendship
those who love you, and those who wounded you,
keeping the tear open,
carrying within oneself at the same time
revolt and sovereign peace,
shedding tears and smiling,
then it may happen
that at the end of our life
a deep song arises.

Jean Sulivan

PREFACE

I met André Daigneault in my late teens, at a time when I dreamed of finding heroes who wanted to do something for humanity. It was the beginning of the sixties, the time when the wind of the "quiet revolution" was sweeping away such beautiful values... André was a young convert in his early twenties, all aflame, like all those young people who, one day, have a profound experience that marks a turning point in their lives. Father Roy, who was recognized for his ease of contact with people, was at the origin of André's true encounter with Christ-Man and God. Deeply involved in the Church as a lay person, André was already in charge of the activities of the magazine "Je crois" ["I Believe" –Ed.]. But he could not disassociate his humanity from his spiritual life, and his poetic creations abounded. Insatiable for knowledge of everything so as to understand human beings better, André was a devourer of books: theology, Goncourt winners, spirituality, psychology, Agatha Christie novels, all types of books that inundated his office when you visited him. Everything that touched human beings interested him.

He was not a priest then, but one could already discern his gift as a communicator and influencer, which made him popular with both the intellectuals and the simplest people. At that time, because I felt that the Church was not close enough to the heart of men (I was largely mistaken), I left my Christian spiritual life. We lost sight of each other for twenty-five years. I studied with the greatest thinkers in psychology and became a psychotherapist. André, for his part, continued to grow in his Christian spirituality and was ordained a priest.

In 1990, as my wife Lise and I came more and more to the evidence that psychology did not have all the answers to the mysteries of human misery and anguish, God came to give us a sign of tenderness, as he knows how to do, for those who sincerely seek him. Lise and I were dealing with the most difficult case imaginable in psychotherapy: a person so hard-hearted that any change seemed impossible. Then one morning when we returned to the office, we found on the steps of the staircase, a book with the striking title: *From a Heart of Stone to a Heart of Flesh*. But, above all, it was the name of the author that really caught our attention: André Daigneault. That this book by a childhood friend who has always remained faithful to God should come into our life at such a tortuous time of questioning could not have been the result of chance. We had just understood that this was a concrete gesture of love coming from God, but our surprise was not at its height. As we opened the first page, we discovered the handwriting of this difficult person who left us a note telling us that she spent all night reading this book and that it had changed her whole life. She had an answer, and so did we through her.

Even after so many years, André had not changed the essentials: he still had his enthusiasm, his sense of humor, his capacity for wonder, with, in addition, a greater wisdom, no doubt acquired at the cost of difficult life experiences.

After reading this new volume from André, *The Long Journey toward Serenity*, we have been touched again as psychotherapists and as Christians. It is a magnificent continuation of *From a Heart of Stone to a Heart of Flesh.* It will reach all who read it, and especially those who have put aside their Christian spiritual life, yet continue to seek meaning in their life. They will find in this volume a new approach to the Gospel, open to human values and humanistic psychology. Fairly simple works remain quite rare (at least in the French language), where one can reconcile the best in the discoveries of psychology with evangelical values and the Christian faith.

As Christian psychotherapists, we will certainly recommend this volume to those we meet in our seminars and in one-on-one interviews. As the author says, we all have to mourn our "idealized image," to discover, as Jung says, our "shadow," and we all suffer more or less, at certain times of our lives, from a sort of neurosis that is not always malignant, but which can become so if we do not have the courage to dive deep into our humanity.

In this volume, psychology and Christian faith come together to tell us the necessary renouncements, acceptances, and surrenders that we must undertake to find, behind our masks, that child of God often a prisoner in the depth of our heart.

With the grace of God (often facilitated by good Christian psychotherapy), this new volume of André could be the beginning or the continuation of this journey within ourselves which it is necessary for acquiring the wisdom to arrive at a true peace of heart and serenity of soul.

Jean-Yves Poirier, M. éd.
Psychotherapist

CHAPTER ONE

TO ACCEPT BEING HUMAN

Man is neither angel nor beast,
and unfortunately,
whoever wants to act the angel acts the beast.
Blaise Pascal

Life is a long journey, a pilgrimage that is pursued through gains and losses, joys and sorrows. This journey begins at birth and ends at the moment of our death. Throughout our existence, we live with losses that propel us, whether slowly or abruptly, to some new stage. We are on a path to recover our heart of a child. We are a people in exodus who undergo various deaths and resurrections.

In fact, the events of our life always ask us the questions: "Where have you come from? Where are you going?" (cf. Gen 16:8). To start out on this path, the first thing that we need to accept is that we are incarnate beings, because the first choice at the beginning of any human growth is self-acceptance, accepting oneself as we are: to accept our reality as it is, with its gifts and weaknesses, with its limitations, woundedness, darkness and final end. Human growth begins when one accepts his own humanity – poor, limited, but also beautiful.

Accepting One's Own Humanity

In spiritual life, there is a subtle but pernicious danger to escape humanity – more or less consciously – in order to take refuge in a world falsely categorized as spiritual. However, life teaches us, sometimes late, that he who wants to act like an angel, sometimes risks acting like a beast. A beast untamed but repressed is always ready to awaken. Is this not an explanation for some colossal falls into sins of the flesh by persons who were found living a rigid but disincarnate asceticism? For a Christian, to reject one's humanity is to reject God. One must not forget this.

We all have the temptation to escape and deny the reality of our humanity by taking refuge in the imaginary or the purely spiritual. Nevertheless, the reality of our humanity is the only means to reach a true Christian spirituality and a measure of emotional stability. In agreement with the spiritual masters, psychologists say that all illnesses of soul and spirit most often involve a certain rejection or disdain of the reality that the human is incarnate. The foundation of humility is, first of all, the acceptance of reality.

Respecting Our "Earthly Side"

The word humility comes from the word "humus." It connects to the word Adam which, in Hebrew, means literally "the earthly," "earth's clay." We need to recognize that we are human, earthly. I would say that we need to consider the "Adam of our being," meaning to respect our human "earthly" dimension.

When man fails to recognize himself as human and "earthly," he collapses. In the Bible, Isaiah foretold the approaching downfall of the inhabitants of Samaria who believed themselves very strong. "From his hand, He will cast them to the ground." Being "cast to the ground" from their throne of pride, these sons of Israel who estimated themselves to be stronger, more important, and better than other people, learned that they were not superior to others. They learned the truth about themselves. As a son of Adam, every human being must, one day, recognize himself as "earthly." The people of God are no exception. The one who does not recognize himself as human and a son of Adam will be cast down. To those who, for whatever reason "believe themselves superior," the Bible says that one day they will collapse and be "cast down." Whoever wants to act like an angel will be surprised to find themselves acting as a beast. Experience shows that the more one elevates himself and becomes hardened, the more difficult the lesson will be through which one will be "cast down."[1]

In Christianity, this is why one speaks of humility. It is first the acceptance of our human condition, the truth about ourselves. Thérèse of the Child Jesus said: "I rejoice in my imperfections." In this way, she gave modern man a true model of humility which is not "idealism" but the recognition of one's fragility and fundamental humanity.

The Seduction of Power

Jean Vanier said:

> The great temptation of a human being is to be seduced by power and to refuse communion with littleness and vulnerability. What is cleanest and purest bursts forth from what is rotten: wine and alcohol come from fermented fruit, and penicillin from gangrene. As the earth is fed by dead leaves and the excrements of animals, so the healing of the heart and our interior divisions become actualized in the measure that we enter into communion with everything that we have rejected and that we are afraid of: the poor, the weak, the stranger. It is a return to earth, clay and mud. Underneath this earth is light. This return is achieved through humility, a word that comes from "humus," earth.

[1] This thought is more developed in the volume of M.A. Santana, *Présence et action de L'Esprit* (Paris: Desclée de Brouwer, 1995).

> A descent to earth is a descent to mud, darkness and the fear of interior wounds.[2]

The denial of our limits and our human reality is the root of pride. I believe that the first step toward human maturity and true humility is to accept ourselves with our limitations, accept that we are incarnate, accept that we are fragile, and accept that we live in a body. "Who wants to act like an angel, acts as a beast," Pascal said with reason. This is why, for the Desert Fathers, sin and humility were more valuable than exterior virtue accompanied by spiritual pride. "Nevertheless, a certain desire of perfection can be a secret desire to be admired, to give satisfaction to parents and circle of friends. It can be a rigid self-will – one believes – to live a high idealism, far above the vicissitudes of ordinary life."[3] Paradoxically, the persons who can admit their fragility show themselves to be of great interior strength, and those who continually want to be strong demonstrate their interior weakness.

Acceptance of one's fundamental humanity and weakness is always a sign of true human and spiritual maturity. It is a fact that each individual has insecurities, wounds, and deficiencies, but some want to hide them by giving the appearance of no failings so that others may believe in their idealized image of so-called perfection. Sadly, one day, the heart and body long repressed will come out and demand their due. The shell will crack and the mask will fall off. At forty or fifty years old, a person can find themselves distressed, defeated, collapsing, and sometimes reacting like a teenager who wants to finally live.[4]

One could also take the example of King David in the Bible. In his middle years he forgot that he was only human and fragile. David, the messianic king, he who had received God's anointing and the holy

[2] Jean Vanier, *Toute personne est une histoire sacrée* (Plon, 1994); Jean Vanier, *Our Journey Home: rediscovering a common humanity beyond our differences* (London: Hodder & Stoughton, 1997).

[3] Jean-François Catalan, S.J., *Dépression et vie spirituelle* (Paris: Desclée de Brouwer, 1996).

[4] André Daigneault, See chapter 1: "De la peur à la confiance" in *Du coeur de pierre au coeur de chair* (Charlesbourg, Québec: Éditions le Renouveau, 1989). —Ed.

oil, this man, too self-assured, became a criminal. He took Uriah's wife and, in order to possess her, sent that military man to be killed. As it were, the "holy" King David, who hid his limits behind his kingly "persona" became obliged to recognize his weakness and his sin. He needed to recognize his humanity and his limits.

God used the prophet Nathan to open his eyes. Since he could not attack the king overtly, he proposed a story:

> *"In a certain town there were two men, one rich, the other poor. The rich man had flocks and herds in great numbers. But the poor man had nothing at all except one little ewe lamb that he had bought. He nourished her, and she grew up with him and his children... she was like a daughter to him. Now, a visitor came to the rich man, but he spared his own flocks and herds to prepare a meal for the traveler who had come to him: he took the poor man's ewe lamb and prepared it for the one who had come to him." David grew very angry with that man and said to Nathan: "As the LORD lives, the man who has done this deserves death! ..." Then Nathan said to David: "You are the man!"* (2 Sam 12:1b-7).

Suddenly, David saw himself in truth. The truth that he was a fragile and weak man. His shell cracked and fell off. His walls crumbled. David became lucid, his eyes opened, and he recognized himself as dust and "earthly." He was as human as others, as limited as others, although he had received God's anointing. He was as much clay as his brothers. He was truly a son of Adam. He recognized his sinfulness.

To recognize one's fragile humanity as an "earthly" creature is often repugnant to us. A mature human being is one who has finally accepted himself. One must know that clear waters are sometimes mixed with polluted water.

Becoming Human through Love

In his book *S'affranchir de la honte*, John Bradshaw writes:

> The Bible suggests that Adam was not satisfied with his own being. He wanted to be more than he was. He desired to be more than human. He failed to accept his essential limitations. . .The Bible suggests that the origin of human bondage (original sin) is the desire to be other than who we are. . .to be more than human. In his pride, Adam wanted a false self. The false self led to his destruction.
>
> Before the fall, the man and the woman were both naked and "were not ashamed" (Gen 2:25). Once they chose to be other than they were, they became naked and ashamed. Nakedness symbolized their true and authentic selves. They were who they were, and they were okay with it. There was nothing to hide. They could be perfectly and rigorously honest. This symbolic and metaphorical description of Adam and Eve is a description of the human condition. Refusing to accept our "real selves," we try to create more powerful false selves or give up and become less than human. This results in a lifetime of cover-up and secrecy. This secrecy and hiding is the basic cause of suffering for all of us. . .Without total self-love and acceptance, we are doomed to the enervative task of creating false selves. It takes tons of energy and hard work to live a false self.[5]

"You will become like gods," said the serpent of Genesis to Adam and Eve. Is not the perennial temptation of the human being to inflate himself, to be what he is not, to deny his humanity and vulnerability? Clearly, this reminds us of the letter of Paul to the Philippians (2:5-11). In this hymn, Paul contrasts the attitude of Christ, the new Adam,

[5] John Bradshaw, introduction to *S'affranchir de la honte* (Éditions Le Jour, 1993); John Bradshaw, *Healing Shame that Binds You* (Health Communications, Inc, 1989).

with that of the first Adam. The latter one wanted to make himself a god by denying his human condition but, on the contrary, Jesus accepted descending and becoming flesh. He immersed himself fully into the human condition in all things. Adam wanted to dehumanize himself, but Jesus humanized himself fully through love. Saint Hildegard said: "The person who is truly holy, first welcomes all that is earthly." Mechthild of Magdeburg also wrote: "Do not despise your body." Meister Eckhart mentioned that the word "humility" comes from the word *humus* or earthly. Therefore, to be humble also means to be in contact with the earth and celebrate our *earthly condition.* Francis of Assisi sang so well about "water our sister," "earth our mother," and "body our brother." A false conception of humility – the one which does not relate to the "earthly" and the "corporal" – denies the child in ourselves and can make us cold and distant human beings under the pretext of spirituality. There are false purities which conceal a hidden pride. Carl Gustav Jung, the psychologist, linked the repression of our human and earthly condition – our fear of mud – to a certain neurosis and the assassination of creativity and life in ourselves. He said: "Real life flows through clear and muddy waters, and too great a "purity" – sometimes in appearance – is lacking in life."

Refusing to Acknowledge One's Own Body

For Man and for a Christian, the great temptation is to disdain the body, to take it into no account, to say to oneself: "I desire pure spirituality, but without an intermediary, without mediation."

Let us not forget that the greatest sin is pride. Saint Thomas of Aquinas said this is why carnal sins are less grievous than the sins of the spirit such as pride, and spiritual pride even more so, because pride is the diabolical sin *par excellence.* To look at the body with disdain is to refuse creation and, since God united himself to a body, it is also to disdain his plan of wisdom and love. A spirituality that would not account for the body, the limits and weaknesses of man incarnate, would not be a true Christian spirituality.

I remember again a word from Simone Weil that, sometime ago, touched me deeply. "It is not in the manner that someone speaks to me about God whereby I perceive that he is filled with the fire of God's love, it is in the way that he speaks to me about earthly realities." In his testament, [Saint] Pope Paul VI spoke these human and splendid words: "I close my eyes on this sorrowful, dramatic and magnificent world."

What Perfection?

To the surprise of many who have idealized them because their "perfection" seemed flawless and almost angelic, how many men and women suddenly collapsed in their forties or even fifties?

An American psychologist who studied the case of hundreds of priests who suddenly left the priestly ministry wrote:

> I have known many priests who left the sacerdotal ministry and I have worked with them; I knew them before and after their departure. Invariably, they were men who gave the least signs that they were going to quit the ministry. At the origin of their departure, it seems that one factor played a role, that of their incapacity to carry their own weaknesses, their fundamental humanity. They were efficacious men who appeared to accomplish and, in fact, did accomplish excellent work. They were concerned about perfection – not in the sense of being driven – but in the sense of a constant, almost perfect, behavior and they almost succeeded. Therefore, it is the proximity to their ideal that prompted people to be astonished at their departure. With a closer look, one realized that these men did not express their true emotional life. Not only were they suppressing their emotions, but they appeared to deny the very existence of them. Their basic human needs were so entirely repudiated as unbearable that they seemed to be deprived of them. Suddenly, their needs pierced through their denial

> and repression. Because of their striving for perfection, they were unable to tolerate the existence of what made them human. By their refusal of human limitations and the reality of incarnate man, they found themselves completely destitute in their forties. [6]

Isn't it for this reason that many spiritual authors consider sins of the *spirit* – such as an arrogant and proud attitude, stubbornness, refusal to forgive, the non-acceptance of one's own weaknesses, along with the refuge into one's "perfectionism" – as the greatest obstacles to God's grace and more serious than the sins of the flesh? Some persons hide behind their apparent perfection and their intellect in order to avoid confrontation with their body and their wounded heart.

> They believe easily that what happens in the mind determines the personality and that this would exclude the fact that the experiences of the body could have an influence on the mind and the behavior. They do not deny having a body, but they consider it only as an instrument of the spirit subjected to the will. Devoid of feelings, their bodily actions are controlled by their image. They need to be perfect and to have others see them as perfect. In reality, in many cases they can display numerous prideful achievements and apparent success, for they often show an ability to get along in the world of power and money. They have a wrong perception of *self*; they are not oriented toward their true selves. On the contrary, their activities tend to validate their image. Their goal is "to appear fine," not to feel fine. They need to assure themselves that no one can have power over them. They are afraid of their feelings and they always control themselves by denying the feelings that risk making them vulnerable. However, they are also obliged to control the situations in which they find themselves. When we think in terms of power,

[6] Robert J. McAllister, "*Journal of Religion and Mental Health*" (July 1975), 335.

there is only one thing to do: fight to acquire more power. Power, however, never overcomes feelings of insecurity and does not soften hidden feelings of humiliation. Power can only deny these feelings. These persons must learn to let go. They must accept their basic humanity. They need to learn to be moved – to be filled with emotions – and even to be overwhelmed by emotional reactions.[7]

The Temptation *par excellence*

The three temptations of Christ are three forms of the same temptation. The temptation of control and power is a primordial and unique temptation over nature, over mankind and kingdoms, and over spiritual strength. The temptation is to "use" the spiritual for one's own glory, to amaze crowds and sustain their admiration. We would desire a *disincarnate* Christianity. This is the first essential temptation that the devil offers Christ: "Be a powerful Messiah instead of a man fragile and weak...! Be almighty and use your power to convince and be admired by the crowds."

This is the real temptation for the Church and Christians, a temptation against which all others pale: *the temptation of power* that desires a God or a Church who sacrifice love for greatness. In the Church, all efforts of true reform will be to reclaim the God of weakness, the God-Child, the God incarnate and defenseless, the God whose authority consists in kneeling at the feet of the poor and the little ones, and accepting a pierced Heart and opened arms in a gesture of love and offering.

Accepting to Be Imperfect

Like Thérèse of the Child Jesus, accepting one's humanity is also accepting to be imperfect, and accepting one's fragility as incarnate

[7] Alexander Lowen, *Narcissism, The Denial of the True Self* (New York: Macmillan Pub. Co.; London: Collier Macmillan, 1983), 152.

man and woman. Our present society, which speaks unceasingly of *excellence*, often compels us to a so-called perfection that is not human, and forces us to build a shell, a persona and an idealized image of ourselves.

In this context, even striving for holiness is not a humble reception of God's gift and His love at the heart of our poverty, but a voluntarist conquest of an ideal that brings us closer to spiritual pride. More than ever, we must remember that, in the spiritual domain, *to excel* is not necessarily to love. *To succeed at any price, to be first, no matter what,* often reveals an old hidden wound.

Winston Churchill said that the individual who constantly tries to succeed was an unhappy child. One must not generalize, but one can say that this was a child loved conditionally, more for his image than for himself. In life, therefore, he receives more pleasure and contentment from viewing himself as acting righteously, rather than actually acting righteously. These persons try to prove their worthiness and, in this way, remain prisoners of their image and their perfectionism.

The French philosopher Henri Bergson once said: "One is sustained by praise and honor to the exact degree that one is unsure of succeeding...However, the one who accepts himself and is confident of lasting works has no need of praise and is above honors, because he creates and knows it, and his joy is a divine joy."[8]

At its origin the perfectionist has deep feelings of insecurity. To combat these feelings, one often builds an idealized image of self. Perfectionism is also often linked to what is called the "Savior complex," which consists of the need to help and save others, in order to safeguard the idealized image as one who never thinks of himself, since he is more occupied with saving others.

[8] Henri Bergson, *L'énergie spirituelle* (Paris: PUFF, 1995), 23-24; Henri Bergson: *l'énergie spirituelle* (Presses Universitaires de France PUFF, 2013).

Karen Horney writes:

> Perfectionist individuals fear that their facade can be recognized as only a facade. In fact, the perfectionist's standards and the quest to achieve them are always linked to a person's pride. It is a false pride that substitutes for true self-esteem. But, whether this pride is false or authentic, the individual is self-satisfied with his virtues and, because of them, feels superior to others. He needs to appear perfect. For him, every failure in his apparent perfection means defeat and danger. He is so inclined to appear perfect and infallible that he must absolutely deny all weaknesses and even problems within himself.[9]

Often, a perfectionist is not conscious of his limitations. That is why he does not know when to stop in his quest for "perfection." In another book, Karen Horney said:

> This brings him a false assurance that appears enviable to all who lack self-esteem. He thinks that he is a benefactor, and that he is magnanimous. This self-perfection is true in some way because he is often admired and the favorite of his parents. During his life, he constantly tries to affirm this self-perception by seeking devotion and admiration.[10]

In the end, perfectionists are victims of their childhood. One cultivates "the values of the perfectionist" in a child by not validating his self-worth. Often, perfectionism starts when love and acceptance by the parents depend on the performance of the child. Then he must constantly surpass himself and go further. There comes a time when he cannot relax nor taste joy or pleasure. He cannot allow himself to simply live and savor good moments.

---

[9] Karen Horney, *Voies nouvelles en psychanalyse* (Paris: Éditions PAYOT, 1976).

[10] Karen Horney, *Neurosis and Human Growth: the Struggle toward Self-Realization* (New York: W.W. Norton Company, 1950).

Karen Horney reminds us of the temptation of Christ to inflate oneself to attain a false perfection and power over others and the world:

> As the years pass, the individual abandons his "true self" to adopt his idealized image. With all his might, he seeks to conform and maintain this image, because – in the depths of this individual – there is self-hatred. An examination of this self-hatred and its devastating force brings us awareness of the tragedy thus presented; it is perhaps the greatest tragedy of the human spirit. In seeking to attain the Infinite and the Absolute, man destroys himself. He makes a sort of a pact with the devil who promises him glory, but he must first descend into hell: hell within himself.[11]

The Temptation in the Desert

As we contemplate his temptation in the desert, we see that Jesus did not renounce his "real self" by turning toward an idealized image, power over all the kingdoms of the world, into which the devil tried to lure him. Resisting this type of temptation and accepting the truth of being incarnate and vulnerable is a sign of true greatness. The struggle that the perfectionist undergoes to conform himself to his idealized image, Karen Horney calls "a pact with the devil," but not in the sense of a willing and conscious diabolical pact, but in the sense of renouncing one's real self, which requires an enormous price: deep alienation of the "real self" and the acceptance of a hidden and secret hell.

This person lives constantly under an interior pressure in order to meet the requirements of inaccessible goals. They need to be perfect because, in fact, it is a self-perfection that they seek to attain. In order to avoid considering their "real self," this person will cultivate a certain pride. Because of it, they will be able to identify with a glorious,

[11] Ibid., 154.

idealized image, and forget the failures of their "real self" – that of an insecure and wounded child – who lives as a prisoner inside of self, and who has so much need to be loved. Thereby, we can understand better the word of Christ who said that, to enter the Kingdom, "one needs to become like a child." The "perfectionist" has great difficulty in becoming a child. They prefer greatness and power. For them, only two solutions remain: *to withdraw and flee, or seeking power to prove their greatness and to never be humiliated.* They do not accept "being like the rest," as mentioned in the Gospel of Luke.

The Search for Power

In refusing to accept their true self and their fragility, this person will always seek admiration. "If I cannot be loved for myself, then I will be admired," they say unconsciously. The desire for admiration is then a substitute for love. The person will aim to be admired by sacrificing the most, by giving the most, by being the poorest, the most perfect, the holiest in the eyes of others, the most understanding, the most charitable, the most spiritual. Whatever! As long as they are admired and "not like the rest of humanity."[12]

[12] As explained by Fr. Jacques Ravanel: "Many people think of joining the divine universe by forgetting themselves in an excessive gift. In reality, they are only running away from themselves and their existence. Far from being perfected, they disintegrate, situating themselves in a vague beyond alongside their person and their life. These people are very demanding of themselves, live according to a rigorous schedule, with an absolute respect of time. They cannot forgive themselves for any mistake or carelessness. Everything is acknowledged based on their cold and rigid reasoning. They inspire more fear than love by building a suffocating and domineering world which cannot bear individuals different from themselves and whose freedom to think appears like a threat. [...] These people are totally self-giving, but with such achievements and vitality that few could emulate this behavior. Their productivity is remarkable, their efficiency formidable, but they remain the center of their activity. The person's own will assumes its promotion in extreme behaviors. These characteristics outline the silhouette of the sublime hero, all the more exceptional in his field and his activity as the appearance is humble. These people worship the perfect, whatever the activity. They are inhabited by the idea of perfection which they project on the world, on things and beings. They think that everything can be dominated and mastered." ("L'Alouette," No. 181, July 1977).

In his book, *La Folie cachée par des hommes du pouvoir*, Maurice Berger explains the ease with which perfectionists fall into narcissism through the fear of accepting their childhood wound.

> Such a subject artificially increases his self-value. He attributes to himself a sort of "super value" that can be described in this way: He is the best (or among the best) or he is of no value, is a nothing.
>
> This feeling of being exceptional is often accompanied by an intense ambition, a constant yearning for power. In meeting with people, he adapts well, with a surprising artificial ease. Behind this easy contact with people, and a brilliant hyperactivity, hides a chronic feeling of emptiness that he fights constantly. In addition to this, there is an enormous dependence on admiration from others. To find himself alone, abandoned, connected to no one, is his anguish. This is why he will act in a way such that he is needed.
>
> This is the question that comes to mind: "Why do we give positions of power to such personalities?"
>
> As mentioned, this man is exteriorly warm, sympathetic and solid. He attracts others by his personality. One thinks he is doing it with "such ease." It must be said that we all have the temptation to imagine that there exists a person that can be strong, intelligent, perfect, devoted to others, and capable of solving all our problems.
>
> The identity of an insecure group is built up momentarily because of him. He presents himself as a group leader; you feel understood and have confidence in him. He seduces you.[13]

[13] Maurice Berger, *La folie cachée par des hommes du pouvoir*, "Pouvoir et Maladie du narcissisme" (Albin Michel, 1993).

His main satisfaction is to be *admired* and his security also depends on this admiration because it gives him the illusion of strength. However, it is a precarious security since every failure or traumatic event can bring to the surface an underlying insecurity beneath the appearance of strength.

In *S'affranchir de la honte*, John Bradshaw explains the search for power and control by wounded persons who have denied their "real self:"

> Throughout my life, I spent my energy watching myself constantly. It was a considerable waste of time and energy induced by the fear of being seen as I was. Had I revealed myself, everyone would have discovered that I was a flawed and defective individual.
>
> The frantic search for power follows the need to control everything. Through the exercise of any power, one tries to compensate for feelings of inadequacy. When one exercises a certain power over others, one is less vulnerable, is less exposed to humiliations. In addition, one can be greedy for power to the point of consecrating his entire life to this search. Under the most neurotic form, this type of greed constitutes an absolute dependency. Some individuals display a folly of energy in elaborating strategies, in shaping intrigues, in playing and maneuvering to climb the ladder of success. Often, they seek to play certain roles or occupy certain occupations in order to obtain the power inherent to these positions, thus hiding their shame.
>
> Individuals striving for power always try to maximize their position by joining with weaker people who are less self-assured and are disposed to be at their service.
>
> The frantic search for power indicates a need to control others. Power constitutes a form of control. Individuals with an imperative need to control everything

> fear being vulnerable. Why? Because, in being vulnerable, they risk humiliations.[14]

The Road to Damascus

There is always a struggle between the idealized self and the real self. Before his meeting with Christ on the road to Damascus, Paul also went astray in this type of illusion; he believed that his idealized image of the Pharisee was within reach and would fulfill his ambition. This is why, after his conversion on the road to Damascus, he spoke so forcefully in his Epistles against seeking an idealized image:

> If anyone else thinks he can be confident in flesh, all the more can I. Circumcised on the eighth day, of the race of Israel, of the tribe of Benjamin, a Hebrew of Hebrew parentage, in observance of the law, a Pharisee, in zeal I persecuted the Church, in righteousness. Based on the law, I was blameless. But whatever gains I had, these I have come to consider a loss because of Christ (Phil 3:4-7).

In these verses, Paul alludes to his past aspirations and the works of his idealized image – "Hebrew born of Hebrew" – and insists on abandoning this image, and on his desire to be his "real self," the only self that matters to Christ.

Often, persons who are prisoners of their *idealized image* can appear strong, with an almost perfect equilibrium. One day something abruptly collapses and they are plunged into depression, which is often surprising to those around them, since this is extremely unexpected from such persons. Suddenly, for various reasons, these persons cannot hide their fragility behind their persona. In the depths of these persons is a refusal of limitations hidden behind the need to be admired or to surpass others.

[14] Bradshaw, *S'affranchir de la honte*, 134-136; Bradshaw, *Healing Shame*.

Thérèse of the Child Jesus and Saint Paul

When considering the spiritual path of Thérèse of the Child Jesus, we realize that it resembles that of Saint Paul – from law to grace.

As with Paul, victory must pass through weakness, setbacks, and the defeat of perfectionism and self- sanctification. On the road to Damascus, Paul is thrown to the ground into the dirt. This is a dramatic reversal. Thérèse of the Child Jesus who, at the beginning, wanted "to become a great saint" and to love as no one had loved before, had to surrender. It is then that she abandoned the work of her sanctification into the hands of Jesus. He is the Savior. This is why Thérèse said: "I desire to appear before him with empty hands."

Additionally, all search for perfection in itself can only engender self-punishment. Faced with the impossibility of matching our brilliant self-image – with which we measure ourselves – and, furthermore, in gazing at the perfect image of Jesus Christ, we can only find ourselves lamenting over the sight of our faults and powerlessness.

As prisoners of this ideal and the exalted motivations that a Christian context brings about, we accuse ourselves constantly. But behind this facade of false humility, hides an insidious and unconscious pharisaism, and a proud attachment to our unrealistic desires. This is why spiritual Masters "consider the search for perfection in itself a demonic narcissism and do not cease to denounce it as a religious trap."[15]

A Spirituality of the Incarnation

In our lives, when there is a separation of the human and the spiritual, we deny that Jesus, in fact, came in the flesh and we, more or less, refuse *the Incarnation* by desiring "to be like gods" and taking refuge in a powerful and infantile self-image.

[15] Philibert Avril, *Épiphanie*, "Délivrez-nous du mal" (Paris: Éditions du Cerf, 1981), 113.

To be able to say: "I am imperfect, I am wounded, I am vulnerable and weak – and God accepts me, so I must accept myself," is a sign of a certain spiritual maturity.

A Guide for Others?

One must accept being *imperfect*, accept being a son for a long time, before becoming a true guide and spiritual father to others. We need to be wary of people who take themselves too seriously and desire to *help us* too much by cultivating their "idealized image." Often, these persons need to dominate through admiration and their false perfection. Nothing reinforces them more than to be a model. If we desire to be a true model as master and spiritual guide, we can observe Saint John the Baptist. He is the true model of a spiritual guide: humble because intelligent, transparent as an imperfect and limited being, and joyful not to be the "Bridegroom," but unaffectedly, "the friend of the Bridegroom." He detaches himself from his own disciples to direct them toward Jesus.

We are all possessive toward those we like to help, and the most dominating of us are those who *think* themselves humble and without expectations from others. To think of oneself as perfect is the worst thing. It is not easy to let go and to free people by detaching oneself. It is not always good to be perceived as a model. Then, others could idealize us and, in this way, oblige us to wear a mask that hides our weaknesses and imperfections. A popular proverb says: "One must not take oneself for another." John the Baptist does not take himself for another. When asked if he were the Christ, he answered: "I am not He. Another one is 'I am.'" As mentioned in Saint John's prologue, the Baptist "is not the Light but came to testify to the Light" (Jn 1:8). Certain persons infatuated by their narcissistic selves – not purified through the nights of the senses and the spirit – believe themselves to be light, and desire that others follow them. Only one is the Christ, only one is the Savior. No one can truly give without having learned to receive for a long time, no one can call himself master if he has not first been a disciple for a long time, no one can claim the right to be obeyed if he himself has not obeyed another. No one can be an adult if he has not first been a true child. No one can become a spiritual father without accepting to be a son for a long time.

John the Baptist said: "You yourselves can testify that I said [that] I am not the Messiah, but that I was sent before him" (Jn 3:28).

This is the authentic joy of a spiritual master, or simply a good therapist, or more simply a good father or mother of a family. As with Abraham, one must accept to *sacrifice* our Isaac, one must refuse to manage others, even our natural or spiritual sons and daughters. One needs to be imperfect and not idealized by others in such a way that they believe us to be the savior of their lives or their group or community. This is the drama of certain founders who, at a certain moment, want to monopolize their community and stop thinking of themselves as "useless servants" whom God desires to use, but who now must disappear so that this child (their community) may grow to mature adulthood. There is grieving when others leave. It is not always easy to accept that the other grows up and might forget us. To accept this without complaining or feeling victimized is certainly a sign of great humility and true spiritual fatherhood. "He must increase; I must decrease" (Jn 3:30), said John the Baptist. One day, possibly, this other that you have helped for many years may not remember all that he owes you, simply because you have done what you needed to do and the other became himself. What you have given him has now become his own good and substance, and not yours anymore. You gave him *life*, and now he must live. The ideal would be that the other does better than ourselves. That is our joy.

To accept that the other *grows up* and becomes himself and that my influence *diminishes* is grief for all fathers, mothers, spiritual guides and priests. What can be said about some of the laity engaged in the Church and in pastoral activities who do not want to *leave* or *let go*, and who, believing that they are indispensable, become more "clerical" than the former clericalism they have spoken of with revulsion and disgust? *Power* is a temptation for all of us, and not only for priests and ordained ministers of the Church.

Is it necessary to mention that a true master has no need to be admired and surrounded? He does not need disciples in order to live, and exists very well without them, since he has found his own identity and does not need others for his existence. The joy of the true spiritual father is that you become yourself and not an extension of him.

More Loving...?

Carl Jung said: "To accept being imperfect is to accept one's "shadow," and accepting to grieve one's idealized image. As long as this shadow is not recognized in ourselves – and scripture, well understood, is suitable for unmasking and illuminating it – we will project this image exteriorly to other people. This shadow is all the evil not recognized in ourselves that we try to eliminate. We can think of those who moralize and, with fury, attack others' weaknesses, especially their carnal sins, because they are afraid to face their own carnal temptations. They feign purity and perfection in fear of accepting impurity and imperfection in themselves.

With age, true spiritual individuals become more flexible, more loving, and even more tender and open to others. They do not harden, they improve. The holy Curé of Ars said: "Saints have a liquid heart."

It is strange to notice that, without being crushed, these persons, fragile but flexible, persevere through many trials and setbacks with no depression or breakdown. The weak become strong, and the "strong and perfect" collapse.

We are all imperfect; we are not the Savior. We are all sinners. With Thérèse of the Child Jesus, we can then rejoice at being imperfect since Jesus has said that he "did not come to call the righteous, but sinners" (Mt 9:13).

The Gentle Earthly Kingdom

One must accept to be *human.* Was Christ less God when he tasted the meals of Martha and Mary and experienced a real, joyful, human moment?

Let us remember that the crowds felt understood in their own language when they heard Jesus speak so simply of harvests, lilies of the fields, nets and fish, goats and sheep. Our temptation will always be to *deny our humanity* and refuse the vulnerability, full of tenderness, of the human Christ. We are *incarnate* human beings and not angels. One must never forget it. "Who wants to be an angel acts like a beast."

In her autobiography, Saint Teresa of Avila said clearly: "We are not angels; we do have a body. To desire acting like an angel on earth is madness...Christ is a very good friend because we see the Man in him; we also see his trials, and he keeps us company."

This is why the spiritual journey necessarily happens through acceptance of the body and the Incarnation. As a principle of true Christian mystical life, one can express that the more an individual is authentically spiritual, the more he becomes incarnate, and the more he becomes really *human.* God becomes flesh and his Eucharistic *body* can heal us from hatred of the body. In this way, Teresa of Avila proclaimed constantly that, even at the summit of contemplation, man has no road other than the Holy Humanity of Jesus, no entry into the Trinity other than the *Flesh* of the Son of Man.

Resetting One's Feet on the Ground

We have a real fear of simply being human. It has been said that true spiritual masters and true saints are more and more *human,* with a scathing sense of humor at times.

Marthe Robin, founder of the "*Foyers de Charité,*" and a great spiritual soul, once received a young intellectual, who was slightly too cerebral. She started talking to him about her garden, her sick lamb, and her tomatoes, to the astonishment of this intellectual who came to meet a "great mystic." Twenty-five years later, laughing like a child, Marthe confessed to him that she purposely spoke of her tomatoes at their first meeting because, she said: "Back then, you were like a frozen statue in a niche. It was necessary to put your feet back on the ground."

Saint Irenaeus said: "The glory of God is man fully alive." One must live and not renounce living. First, we must accept our humanity, our affections, our body. There is no real chastity where there is fear of sexual reality. There is no true humility where there is fear of affectivity, and fear of accepting one's own life. Behind certain virtues it is easy to detect some type of "barrier," some "tension or a desire to be admired."

In my book, *Les Carnets du Soir*, I write:

> He believes that he has a religious vocation because he is afraid of life. He believes that he should enter into a community because he needs security. He believes that he lives in poverty because he never managed finances. He believes that he lives in obedience because he is afraid of giving his opinion. He believes that he lives in chastity because he fears sexuality. He believes that he loves everyone because he does not love someone. He believes that he is open to God because he is closed to humans. He believes that he is faithful and persevering because he does not have the courage to leave the community that took care of him. He believes that he lives a spiritual childhood because he has become childish with authority. He believes that he lives the dark nights of the soul of the great mystics because he feels misunderstood...He is neurotic and ignores it, but believes himself to be a great spiritual soul.[16]

[16] André Daigneault, *Les carnets du soir* (Charlesbourg, Québec: Les Éditions Le Renouveau, 1993).

Based on "forgetfulness of self," certain commitments and sacrifices can result in surprising catastrophes. Fear of living can sometimes hide behind a rejection of the world. Jesus Christ said:

"Love your neighbor as yourself." Let us note that he never said: "Love your neighbor instead of yourself." This is very different.

The long journey toward serenity, and human and Christian maturity, starts primarily with the acceptance of our basic humanity, of this "earthly" being that we all are, and by the rejection of that persona that we have fabricated a little at a time to protect the wound in our heart of a child. "I am not like the rest of humanity," said the Pharisee of the Gospel. "You will be like gods," said the serpent of Genesis. As mentioned by Claude Dagens, in *Eloges de notre faiblesse [Praise for Our Weakness]*: "Holiness begins where the obsession of perfection ends – the simple discovery that we are weak human beings in need of love and assistance. True joy does not consist in striving toward super-human perfection but, to the contrary, in accepting the limitations of one's humanity. One who dreams of perfection, without succeeding, is inevitably hard on himself and, consequently, hard on others."

The beginning of a real human and Christian spirituality is our acceptance of being flesh and blood – incarnate – the acceptance of reality and our own limitations. We cannot give ourselves to others if we have not found and accepted ourselves in our wounded humanity.

Saint Bernard himself repeated to the pope whom he counselled: "Take care of others, but do not forget yourself."

Ballad

Forgive me if I dare speak to you once again
With the simple words of my childhood
With the simple flowers that decorate the fields
Forgive me if I dare to have a heart

When my flesh is stirred in the month of May
With the white lilacs and maple sap
With the words of love that spin in my head
Forgive me if I dare to have a heart

Forgive me for believing in my sun
That a rose is more lovely to sing than a chant
That only one word suffices to discover joy
Forgive me if I dare to have a heart

Forgive me madam to have written these verses
They are useless and meaningless
But if tomorrow a child weeps upon reading them
Forgive me tonight if I dare to have a heart

CHAPTER TWO

ACCEPTING ONE'S OWN SOLITUDE

No one can live with others
unless he is first able to live alone.
Moussa Nabati

The psychologist Erich Fromm said that the capacity to appreciate one's own solitude is the condition *sine qua non* to truly love others. As long as you are not comfortable with yourself, as long as you cannot appreciate moments of solitude, you cannot love another except by necessity.

In a strange way, the people happiest in their moments of solitude, are those whose relationships with others flourish the most; those who are not comfortable with themselves find it difficult to question the quality and quantity of their human connections.

One day, close to depression, a German priest asked for a meeting with Carl Jung, the great psychoanalyst, for some help, as he could not live under the pressure of his fourteen-hour work day. Jung counselled him this way: "If you want to get better, you will need some lifestyle changes. You will need to work an eight-hour day, rest in the evening, and then remain by yourself until bedtime. The priest expressed his gratitude by saying: "I will do everything that you have requested because I want to be healed." The next day, he cancelled his appointments, worked eight hours, ate his dinner, and retired to his living room. There, he became anguished and agitated. So he listened to Chopin and finished a novel from Herman Hesse. The next day, he repeated the same schedule, apart from this time listening to Mozart and starting a novel from Thomas Mann. At bedtime, this educated and cultivated man, nevertheless, felt as poorly as before.

The next morning, he returned to Dr. Jung and told him somewhat belligerently: "I followed your counsel but I do not feel better." He described his evenings. Jung looked at him attentively and said: "You seem to have misunderstood. I did not want you to be in the company of Chopin, Hesse, Mozart or Mann. I wanted you to be alone: alone with yourself." To this, the priest replied: "Oh! Doctor, I cannot think of worse company!" Jung then gave him a cutting but true remark: "But it is the same company you inflict on others fourteen hours a day!"

Evidently, Jung saw clearly that the problems of his client were due to a lack of intimacy and fear of aloneness. This is the question that can be asked: As with many of us, why was this responsible man struggling with looking into the depths of his heart?

The Fear of Not Being Accepted

We all have the fear of facing ourselves because, in our depths, we do not believe in our value. Many men and women are workaholics and cannot stop, because they cannot believe that they can be loved for themselves.

To be alone and accept one's solitude is the foundation and a new stage of growth. We are all afraid of the conflict that might be revealed in our solitude. It is about facing our limitations, our woundedness, and refraining from taking refuge in our activity, even if it be charitable or apostolic. Before Jacob's name was changed to Israel, he had to live in *solitude* and wrestle the *stranger* who fought with him during the night. "Jacob was left there alone. Then a man wrestled with him until the break of dawn. When the man saw that he could not prevail over him, he struck Jacob's hip at its socket, so that Jacob's socket was dislocated as he wrestled with him" (Gen 32:25-27).

We are all fearful of meeting this *stranger* in the solitude of the night because we are afraid that something could "disconnect" within ourselves, that our "persona" and our idealized image would be defeated and destroyed and that this *stranger* in ourselves – "this Israel," "this prince with God," "this child of God," in ourselves – would reclaim its rights. This is why we have such a need to be surrounded by others and admired, that we sometimes panic when, facing ourselves, we find ourselves alone. Behind our mask, our commitments, and multiple activities – which give the impression that we are somebody – lies this fragile child that, in the depths of our heart, wants to live.

After facing and accepting our solitude, we become more able to live with others without "conformity" or having the need to *save* or *dominate*. We are then capable of true intimacy since we are reconciled with our true self, and with this child of God, this Israel in ourselves who desires to live fully. "You shall no longer be named Jacob, but Israel." (Gen 32:29).

Some people have great difficulty entering their solitude, because they fear grieving the loss of their "persona" and their "idealized image." They refuse to wrestle, and they prefer their facade to their real self.

In his volume, *Gagner à en mourir*, Alexander Lowen writes:

> The existence of a facade betrays the fact that this person functions as an image rather than his real self. A facade is observed by a frozen expression such as a permanent smile on the face. A facade is really a mask characterized by a lack of life. Another indication is a special look in the eyes or rather an absence of expression. The eyes are dim. They express nothing. This flatness of the eyes does not

> reflect a dullness of spirit. On the contrary, intellectually, these persons are alert and lively; they think clearly and logically. Their thoughts, however, are not connected to their feelings. It appears that their heart is not alive.[17]

At a moment in time, especially in their forties, men and women need to enter into their *solitude* and face their woundedness. It is the struggle between their persona and their real self who, like a child who has been suffering for a long time, finally wants to live.

To Stop Denying

In facing our problems, there is no other solution than to enter into our solitude by refusing to deny our woundedness and fragility, and accepting to wrestle with our Jacob. Let us have a closer look at this Biblical passage. It is dark. Jacob is *alone.* He is afraid. Then he is attacked by a *stranger.* A parallel with the struggle of middle age is quite clear. Alone and disoriented in the middle of the night, Jacob wrestles with this stranger. This wrestling in the night has a consequence: "He struck Jacob's hip at its socket, so that Jacob's socket was dislocated as he wrestled with him" (Gen 32:26). In this solitude and this combat during the night, Jacob will be changed. He will accept to be wounded. He will get up..."Jacob limped along because of his hip" (Gen 32:32).

Is this not our story? We either escape our solitude by taking refuge in our activities – then we regress toward an immaturity hidden under the appearance of strength – or we engage in our struggle in mid-life, enter our solitude, and recover our true identity. "You shall no longer be named Jacob, but Israel" (Gen 32:29).

We must accept to limp, accept *to be imperfect,* accept to be wounded, and accept our fundamental aloneness.

[17] Alexander Lowen, *Gagner à en mourir* (Hommes et Groupe Éditeurs, 1987).

Fear of Solitude

Each individual is alone in life. We are born alone and we die alone. Each is alone in the sense that no one can be born, grow, increase, and desire in the place of someone else. We are all unique and irreplaceable. Unfortunately, many people want to escape from their solitude. To them, aloneness represents motherly abandonment and lack of love. They always have the need to be embraced and admired. They feel that they can exist and live only by clinging to others and being admired by them. It is as if they are nothing without the gaze and support of others. They remain dependent. Therefore, they are incapable of living a true intimacy with someone. In fact, it is impossible to establish a real friendship or love another unless we can first enter our own solitude. Moussa Nabati said: "No one can live with others unless he is first able to live alone," meaning with a separate identity, not conforming and dependent on the identity of others.

In the Bible, when God orders Abraham: "Go forth from your land, your relatives, and from your father's house to a land that I will show you" (Gen 12:1), he did not condemn him to wander. On the contrary, he encouraged him to *become himself* in the sense that, to go toward self, to become real, and to accept aloneness, presupposes a cut, a break, and being uprooted. It is about finding one's true identity *apart* from the paternal home. It requires a renunciation of conformity. "Leave your father's house..." but "go forth to a land that I will show you," that is, find your true identity apart from your surroundings and distinct from social conformity and your role. Find yourself beyond your persona and role. Do not be dependent on paternal images. It is a matter of entering into maturity and accepting solitude. It is an invitation to be alone, to follow a *personal* path different from others and even different than family opinion. "Go to yourself, for yourself," and do not fear solitude. Therefore, to be alone signifies that I am myself, different than you and, for this reason alone, the connection with others becomes possible, since I do not have the need to please others or be admired in order to be somebody.

Accepting Rejection from One's Family

In the Gospel, there is a passage that no one seems to notice, yet is nevertheless *astounding*, because it is very contrary to what we may think of Jesus' relationships with his family and relatives. This event takes place at the beginning of Jesus' public ministry. It happens in Capernaum, a village of fishermen near the Sea of Galilee, about forty kilometers from Nazareth where Jesus grew up.

"He came home. Again [the] crowd gathered, making it impossible for them even to eat. When his relatives heard of this, they set out to seize him, for they said, 'He is out of his mind'" (Mk 3:20-21).

Let us notice that the exegesis writers were generally *silent* on this passage where Jesus' family, his relatives and his cousins, are ashamed of him and want to seize him, because Jesus dishonors them by acting the way he does. They are not proud to have someone like him in their family and do not "idealize him." On the contrary, they would like to *hide* him and to seize him because "he is out of his mind." A little further, in verse 32: "Your mother and your brothers [and your sisters] are outside asking for you." But Jesus responds unhurriedly: "Who are my mother and [my] brothers?"

Jesus is not seeking to please and to comply with the *expectations* of his family. One could even think that he does so on purpose. During all his public life, there is only one visit to his village of Nazareth that is spoken of. Truly he does not seek the admiration of his relatives. Moreover, this one and *only* visit reveals itself to be a fiasco, since the reception by the people of his village is so hostile that Jesus is unable to do what he has done in other cities. "He came to what was his own, but his own people did not accept him" (Jn 1:11). Here we also see that his relatives and his cousins were among those who "did not believe in him" (Jn 7:5).

Jesus was approximately thirty years old when he returned to his village where his family said: "He is out of his mind." From the beginning of his public ministry, Jesus truly separated himself from his family and asked his disciples to do the same. When one knows how important it was in this era to bury one's dead, especially one's parents, we are surprised, if not scandalized, in Jesus' response to the young man who asked him: "[Lord,] let me go first and bury my father" (Lk 9:59). "Let the dead bury their dead" (Mt 8:22).

In another passage, Jesus said that, to pursue one's personal mission, one must risk provoking division around oneself: "Do you think that I have come to establish peace on the earth? No, I tell you, but rather division" (Lk 12:51). He added that one will have people from "one's own house" as enemies. It is not easy to become oneself, to extract ourselves from parental influences that can attempt annexation by enticing us to become the person of their dreams and not what we have dreamed of for ourselves.

François Chirpaz makes us understand how much the desire for security can prevent someone from being independent and different from his parents' expectations.

> A child is not his father, he is not his mother, and can live his life only by accepting to be neither, but only himself, in daring to leave the orbit of one or the other parent. The search for security remains infantile until one refuses to live in the parental orbit. He desires to affirm himself and wants to shake off the guardianship. He dares to assert himself differently from the wishes of his father or mother. At the same time, because of his affective immaturity, he is afraid of this difference (because this experience is the one of solitude) and he even refuses it and denies it in his imagination. He wants to remain in the parental orbit in order to preserve the security and admiration of his parents. He refuses to be other than the desire of his parents for him and does not accept to be different in their eyes. He is afraid to leave the parental orbit because he fears the unbearable

suffering of solitude by crushing the image that his parents have made for him.[18]

Comparing this text to the Gospel, it is clear that Jesus was a *free* man who did not answer to the *expectations* of his family and relatives. Like Abraham his ancestor, he truly dared to leave the *paternal* home and the familial orbit to be faithful to himself and his mission. Humanly and psychologically, he was a mature and independent man, who had no need to *please* his parents and relatives in order to portray an image of a good son and an exemplary cousin. "He is out of his mind" (Mk 3:21), they said of him. Jesus was truly different from us. He did not fear being alone. He embraced his solitude. He is an example of interior freedom.

If we have not found our own identity and have not left our paternal home, we are very dependent on others. The "other" is successively *idealized* or *demonized*. One expects from the other that he fulfill all our dreams and take care of us. One expects from the other the realization of our wishes and demands. However, after some years, one regrets it because it ceases to correspond to our infantile expectations of an ideal father or mother, or of that person who will finally arrange everything to provide us with security. One will move easily from transfer to counter-transfer. To the extent that someone was a god for me, he will become a demon.

An individual who has not found his identity and has not accepted his solitude will be very permeable to sectarian cults and to the influence of a leader or guru. It is in this sense that, in their forties or fifties, certain persons can be found still seeking an ideal father or mother who will take care of them and control their life instead of them caring for themselves.

[18] François Chirpaz, *Difficile rencontre* (Paris: Éditions du Cerf, 1982), 59.

Solitude and Openness

True solitude is the opposite of isolation. Isolation closes oneself, but solitude opens up to others. In the Bible, the solitude of the desert is always the prelude to a mission, a new stage, a new vocation.

Our life is permeated with crises, passages, transitions and exoduses. For us, the exodus of Moses and the people of Israel is an example and is symbolic. This *passage* demonstrates specific characteristics of a crisis of human and religious transition.

The intolerable conditions in Egypt led Moses and the people to flee into the solitude of the desert. Therefore, there is a movement toward a new period, or a new mission in life. First, the situation became intolerable, then came a phase of misery, followed by the acceptance of solitude and, afterward, entrance into new life, a new stage and, at times, a new mission within the same tradition, but different than the first period.

During the stage of the desert and solitude, we often live with doubts and painful nights. Some people do not attain the "promise land" and die in the "desert" of their solitude. In the Bible, we see that, among the adults who fled Egypt in the beginning to enter into the desert, only two men arrived at their final destination. Many were unsuccessful in completing the "passage" and it was their children who pursued the realization of their dreams.

Often we are afraid of the "middle-age transition" because we refuse to mourn the dreams of our youth and the illusions of the teen years.

In the desert of our solitude, we must die to ourselves, die to the narcistic desire to please, to charm and to always seek the esteem of others. In the volume *La Quête de L'Identité chez François d'Assise: de Narcisse à Jesus*, Jean-Marc Charron speaks to us about the narcistic features of Francis before his conversion, and how his development will bring death to narcissism:

> We find a search for admiration at work in the life of Francis. A narcistic individual, obsessed with the desire to succeed, and seeking the esteem of others, often becomes a charmer; he creates his relationships through seduction. In this way, we often find him with the appearance of a man courteous, kind, and "well educated." He is well mannered and seems always preoccupied with the well-being of others. In his behavior, this individual, in fact, seeks public approval. It is this trait of a narcistic personality that we find in what has been reported of the young Francis.[19]

The young Francis was always afraid of being alone. He constantly needed to be surrounded by friends who admired him. Celano, one of his biographers, explains: "Superior to his friends, he was their performer and dazzled them all. From there, his reputation grew throughout the province to the extent that those who knew him said that he would become someone great."

To become someone great, to charm and seduce, to be admired and surrounded, to appear mild-mannered, to care for the well-being of one's circle of friends, and to gain approval from everyone, is the image of narcissism which, to a certain extent, applies to young Francis before his conversion, because he was unable to enter into himself and live his solitude. We know how much young Francis was loved by his mother, but he did not have much of a relationship with his father whom he feared.

Speaking of the masculine narcistic profile, Alice Miller writes:

> He is the favorite son of his mother. This child needs to be admired. He needs to brilliantly succeed in his enterprises and achieves them. (However, he never undertakes what he is unsure of succeeding at.) In this way, he admires himself for his qualities, his intelligence, his talents, his successes and performances.

[19] Jean-Marc Charron, *De Narcisse à Jésus: la quête de l'identité chez François* d'Assise (Montréal: Paulines, 1992). —Ed.

And Alice Miller adds:

> They succeed in all their undertakings, sometimes even in an extraordinary fashion. They are admired and envied, they are successful where they want to be, but all this is to no avail. Depression, a feeling of emptiness, the impression of self-alienation and the absurdity of life lie in wait and invade them as soon as the drug of "grandiosity" fails them, as soon as they are not ON TOP, they are not headliners, or not at the height of the idealized image they have created for themselves. They fall prey to anguish, shame and feelings of guilt.[20]

They succeed in almost all their endeavors but, at the same time, they are extremely fragile under their shell.

For these persons, the journey toward maturity and holiness must pass through the acceptance of their wounded heart of a child. Life and trials must shake them and throw them off their pedestal, much like Saint Paul on the road to Damascus, who became blind and had to be led by the hand like a child.

In the saints who advanced toward holiness, one always notices an entrance into solitude and a collapse before a deep change. One sees this in the young Francis of Assisi. He needed illness in order to change radically and to stop searching for "social success." When the pope asked him facetiously to "rather roll in manure with the pigs" and Francis obeyed like a child, he started to die to his pride and to his primary narcissism. He definitely separated from his parents who did not, then, regard him in the same way. His father was ashamed of him and his mother remained silent but withdrew herself more and more from his life.

[20] Alice Miller, *Le drame de l'enfant doué: à la recherche du vrai* soi (Paris: P.U.F., 1983); Alice Miller, *The Drama of the Gifted Child: the Search for the True Self* (London: Faber and Faber, 1983).

Alice Miller explains:

> He knows that as long as he is admired for his qualities, he is not loved for who he really is. Behind the pride of parents who are given such a gifted child is, dangerously close, the shame that these parents feel if this child does not fulfill their expectations any longer.[21]

Certain individuals who do not live a teenage crisis, then have more difficulty entering the middle-age transition and mourning the illusions of youth and their grandiose dreams. Only a true conversion, a metanoia, a change of mentality, and acceptance of solitude can bring them toward a new stage of life.

Some people can arrive at this stage by a failure, an illness, a great suffering, or even a depression – when all the artifices and surroundings of their life crumble away – when they accept, in the depth of their wounded heart, this child of God who wants to live and be loved unconditionally. Then the entrance into solitude becomes the beginning of a long journey that will lead toward serenity.

[21] Ibid.

I Go through Nights

I go through nights dying of pain
Broken is my heart and torn is my soul
I travel through nights extending like days
Too long to groan and too dark for my veins

I go through nights like a long corridor
Alone like a white pebble at the bottom of a big black lake
I go through nights like a death
That pierces my soul and hurts me and bites me

And I don't stop bleeding of tenderness
And I don't stop diving into my pain
Yet in this agony and this Mass offered
I beg you my God to tear out my heart

CHAPTER THREE

ACCEPTANCE OF SELF

One must reject falsehood and illusions,
and see reality the way it is.

Erich Fromm

The path toward the truth about ourselves is often arduous and difficult. It is not easy to accept ourselves and accept others. How many people, including ourselves, live a falsehood more or less consciously? They hide under all types of pretenses and defense mechanisms. Their life becomes a sort of masquerade, a game of hide and seek, and they exhaust themselves denying and repressing their wounds by not accepting themselves. They appear to have a great personality – charitable, generous and indispensable – in the eyes of others.

Instead of facing reality and accepting ourselves, we often prefer to flee from the wounded child in us by an outpouring of activity which increases our value, or by sickness: anxiety, backaches, insomnia, ulcers, angina, various tensions, etc. One day, we will need to face our old wounds and become true to ourselves and to others because, without this, we will always present a false-self and a facade to others. What repressed aggression and violence can be discovered, for example, behind the facade of individuals who wear a *perpetual smile*?

It is remarkable how we can lie without noticing it. We say "yes" to a person fearing to displease them when, deep down, we desire to say "no." We respond quickly that "all is well," fearing any more personal questions that would make us uncomfortable. Or we say, "I have no time," in order not to answer, "I do not want to," and thereby losing our idealized image of a good and generous person.

Unfortunately, we are often prisoners of our "idealized image." We are uneasy when meeting a transparent person who is without a mask because it unsettles us. At the core, instead of accepting ourselves in our human weakness and accepting reality as it is, we prefer denying our fragility and we *idealize* others.

We have a great need to idealize someone. In the Gospel, when the young man approached Jesus and called him "good master," the response of Christ was surprising: "Why do you call me good? No one is good but God."

It is remarkable to see the wisdom of Christ since these first words addressed to the young man foil the temptation by which this young man seeks in Jesus an ideal father, and therefore, also builds in himself the false image of a perfect son.

This brings us to the line in a theater play, *Le Malade Imaginaire*: "Mister, you are good!" "No, I am not good; I am bad whenever I want to be!" These well-known lines that Molière places in his hypochondriac's mouth express a great truth. It is not that easy to simply be good..."*God alone is good*" as we are reminded in the Gospel; no man is ever simply good. Regarding a man who always smiled with an unfailing kindness, a psychologist said: "What type of aggression and violence is hiding within him in order to always appear so gentle and mild?"

Some individuals want to "appear good" and hide their aggressiveness and their lack of confidence under a smile and false generosity, whereas others, who appear to be of less goodness, often manifest a true generosity.

The Bible reports:

> *"A man had two sons. He came to the first and said, 'Son, go out and work in the vineyard today.' He said in reply, 'I will not,' but afterwards he changed his mind and went. The man came to the other son and gave the same order. He said in reply, 'Yes, sir,' but did not go"* (Mt 21:28-30).

Where is authentic goodness and generosity? Where do we find the most sincere attitude, one that manifests itself as a true desire to serve? Appearances are often deceiving. True goodness is not always where one might find it at first. Thérèse of the Child Jesus said: "I love only the truth, I abhor pretenses." I understand her when I meet Christians who always smile as if they were obliged to *look happy.* Once Jesus said that "his soul was sorrowful unto death," and the Evangelist added that "he was filled with anguish and distress." I prefer the example of Jesus to the absurd and feigned smile of some Christians who think of evangelizing in this way. I do not know if these persons have made a "vow" of happiness, but I would much prefer a vow of being constantly oneself and to admit to sadness unto death at times. Truly, I cannot suffer sugary language and those ridiculous smiles that deny an incarnation into weakness and the reality of the human condition. The false joy and the forced smile often hide an enormous weight of repressed aggression and violence. It is good that the Bible reminds us of the psalmist who is unafraid to express his weariness, his sadness, and his revolt:

> *My heart is withered, dried up like grass, too wasted to eat my food.*
> *From my loud groaning, I become just skin and bones.*
> *I eat ashes like bread, mingle my drink with tears* (Ps 102:5-6, 10).

> *I rock with grief;*
> *I groan at the uproar of the enemy, the clamor of the wicked.*
> *They heap trouble upon me, savagely accuse me.*

My heart pounds within me; death's terrors fall upon me.
Fear and trembling overwhelm me; shuddering sweeps over me
(Ps 55:3b-6).

The men of the Bible are not afraid of their negative emotions. They shout their anxiety, their anguish, and their troubles, without shame, and this is wonderful for us. I am not against joy or a smile provided that this joy emerges from *the heart,* and becomes spontaneous in the eyes and on the lips. I am not sure why, but I often guess a restlessness behind false smiles and fictitious joy. And do not tell me that these absurd smiles and superficial joy are from charity. I do not believe that. Is not false goodness an escape that we refuse to see? One seeks to create the self-image of a good and generous person in order to be appreciated. Sometimes this generosity is an escape. There is a type of goodness and generosity that comes from a desire to be first, to "succeed" in the sphere of endeavors and virtue. One works at many things but this activity does not always come from the heart. It arises rather from the need to be appreciated and admired. This can provide an individual a profound interior tension. These persons burn out quickly. In their mid-forties or fifties, they sometimes arrive at a point of fatigue and exhaustion whereby they break physically or psychologically. However, they still find contentment since it is said about them: "What is there to say, he worked so hard; she was so generous!" Then, instead of searching for the true source of *exhaustion,* one is content to be *admired* because one broke down after so much *work.* Let us not forget that the word *exhaustion* means, first of all, that the well is empty. These individuals do not want to recognize that their need to be a "savior" is a classic narcissistic compensation. They lack true humility.

Where can true goodness and true generosity be found? I think that there is a *false* goodness which is hyperactivity; one runs to help others, but one refuses to look at, and accept, one's own poverty and woundedness.

Embracing One's Own Poverty

Referring to Jesus' words, Carl Jung said that he found it marvelous that Christians discover Jesus in the poor. "I was hungry and you gave me to eat, I was thirsty and you gave me to drink...and what you did to the least, you did to me." However, he could not understand that Christians, too often, avoided their individual poverty; that they did not recognize Jesus in their own poverty. Can one really help the poor and the wounded if one does not first embrace one's own poverty and brokenness?

If one does not love himself, if one always desires to be admired, then can they truly help?

This is the thought of Jean Vanier:

> In order to help another in making the necessary effort to grow, one must not be a prisoner of emotions, fearing to upset, fearing to be separated. To love is desiring that the other grows toward a great freedom. It implies firmness and even anger. One must not possess the other at all cost. One must sometimes direct the other toward someone else who can help them with more competence. In truth, to love, one must cease to always please and must accept to be left out. The first thing needed to really help is to primarily stop evading our own woundedness.[22]

The Helper Syndrome

What is our motivation in helping others and counselling them? A German psychotherapist, Schmidbauer, gave evidence of what he calls "the helper syndrome" whereby the motivations in counseling and helping others were numerous and often, unconsciously, centered on a desire or need to *control*. Deprived of love and acceptance in childhood, some individuals search for approval as compensation from

[22] Jean Vanier, "Vraie et Fausse Bonté," CHRISTUS, No.128.

their clients and their directees. In this black hole of a lack of love, hides "power." It confirms the judicious remark from Jung: "Where love is missing, power occupies the empty space." [23]

A counselor, a psychologist, or even a spiritual director, who absolutely wants to *direct*, ends up, as it is sometimes said, building a facade with the persons they are meeting with. As mentioned by the Swiss psychoanalyst Guggenbühl, the more an individual is persuaded that he is working for altruistic motives, the more a shadow of power increases. Jung speaks of the *mask* of certain counselors. But the desire for power, that a counselor wants to hide and repress under the beautiful idea of "doing good to someone," nevertheless does not cease to exist. Some indications can reveal its existence: the sorrow felt when leaving his client or his directee by referring them to someone else when he has reached the limits of his competence, the difficulty of accepting critical views, jealousies and tensions with others who also care for one of his patients or his directees, etc.

The first step in healing from one's desire for power is to *admit it*. Admitting one's pride is always the beginning of true humility, accepting ourselves in our wounded humanity. If we have not accepted our weakness, if we have not accepted ourselves as we are in our fragile being, then we will flee our vulnerability and we will try to forget our poverty by desiring to *help* others. As Jean Vanier has said: "It is a very deep egoism – hidden under generosity – this desire to be first in the field of love and virtue. This subtle spiritual egoism urges a person to success. At its limits, it uses the poor to *prove* and cultivate one's own image." This is not true goodness.

[23] "How does this need for power come about which, in many people, is not directed against other people but against themselves? The lust for power is a substitute for pent-up love. The man who cannot enjoy the greatest pleasure, that of being loved, compensates for this lack by the exercise of power. The latter contains an element of revenge: since you don't love me, I control you!" *Jésus le guérisseur*, Helmut Jaschke (Paris: Éditions Brepols, 1997), 54.

Give Me a Drink

Let us look at the attitude of Jesus toward the Samaritan woman in John's Gospel. In front of this poor woman, wounded in her heart and soul, Jesus did not initially tell her: "I came to do some good for you." At first, he did not give her any advice. He simply said: "Give me a drink." Jesus adopts the attitude of a poor one and of a beggar. He expresses his own needs. "Give me a drink," he said, and not, "I come to give you some good advice to help you and to save you," but rather, "give me a drink." And instead of presenting himself to this woman as someone who gives, who helps, who brings about, in other words, who is superior, Jesus presents himself as the one in need of her. To this poor woman, Jesus does not give gratuitously, offering his service, but asks for a little favor. Jesus exposes his own needs. He says: "Give me a drink."

Jesus demonstrates what true love and true goodness is. He shows us that to love is not first *to do something* for someone, because one can do many things for another in order to dominate them, and render them more dependent on our generosity and so-called goodness. One can appear to love others in order to increase and valorize oneself. One can even engage in ministry in order to believe that one is good since he does so many things for people who have nothing. This is not loving. To love someone is not to be generous; to love someone is not organizing things for them; to love someone is not to *lean over* someone to help them from the height of our generosity and virtue; to love someone is to reveal their goodness which is unique, and affirm their gifts. It is also accepting to receive from them and not only to give. At its core, true love does not dominate; it does not frighten; it makes itself small to give life and, at the same time, accepts receiving. In front of his apostles, Jesus presents himself as poor and little. When I read the Gospel, I understand Peter so well when Jesus is kneeling in front of him. He says: "No, you will not wash my feet." I imagine that most of us would say the same thing. We have such difficulty *receiving* and letting ourselves be loved in our poverty and weakness. Jesus, poor, humble and kneeling, washes feet. Basically, we do not like this type of authority because it lacks dignity. Jesus who washes feet becomes poorer and smaller than we are. It is the mystery of true love. True love does not dominate and does not seek admiration; it does not frighten, it makes itself small like a helpless child. This gesture of Jesus naturally disturbs us.

That I would live like this! Before washing others' feet (which could easily become a performance), I need to acknowledge my own dirty feet and, like Peter, accept to receive, to be helped, to have my feet washed, and surrender my weakness and misery. Without this, I would play the *benefactor*. Jean Vanier has said:

> Sometimes there is an attraction to the poor or the weak because one can dominate; one needs to help them. We all know that our loving gestures, our goodness and our idealism can be tarnished by seeking ourselves in the need to help, to dominate, to be right. This is pride. It is in the area of charity that one can most live in the illusion of virtue and pharisaism. It is a great danger for the *professionals* of charity.[24]

We love poorly. We desire to teach the other, to help the other, but in our own way, for ourselves. The power instinct is sometimes reinforced by the feeling of having given to others. There is nothing worse than the pride of a person who thinks of themselves as *good* and disinterested, who spends themselves on others because these others feel guilty if they separate themselves from the helper. There is nothing worse than meeting a savior who thinks of themselves as *The Savior*.

Alexander Lowen wrote:

> A savior is an individual whose structural characteristics render him available to others, responding to their needs, sometimes at his own expense. The physical structure of

[24] Jean Vanier, "Compatir," CHRISTUS, No.111.

> a savior is extremely rigid. He cannot afford a breakdown because others count on him. His shoulders are straight and tense and he is convinced that he must carry the weight of others' problems. One distinctive trait of this type of personality is the inability to ask for help; this indeed, would be admitting weakness and need. A savior rarely weeps.[25]

To love truly, one must accept to be oneself without a mask or a shell. To truly love, one cannot be possessive or domineering. True Love is always humble and vulnerable. To be humble is to say, like Jesus to the Samaritan woman: "Give me a drink," to receive from others and the poor. We think that we love, we believe ourselves to be good, but too often, *we find our security* in the power we exert on others under the appearance of goodness. "Give me people to help, give me some good to be performed because, without it, I will experience anxiety and will need to face my fundamental insecurity." Adrian van Kaam explains how some wounded individuals, through entrance into religious life and the hierarchy of the Church, can sometimes seek power for the sake of power:

> If I fear facing my anxiety, I may seek for power within the religious organization of which I am a member, as a layman, a priest, or a religious. I may crave power for its own sake, not for the sake of the religious community or of the faithful. Moreover, my personal spiritual life may be marked by my addiction to power...My dedication to the religious cause becomes dependent on its power to increase my hold on myself and on others. I am very careful about the nature of my religious occupation. I avoid under many pretexts any work that would not lead to an increase in my power or prestige...The neurotic religious person is also frequently

[25] Alexander Lowen, *La peur de vivre* (Paris: Épi, 1983), 76.

> tempted to surround himself with persons of like mind. His *religious* love for people exists only if they can satisfy his need to be admired, loved, and adulated.[26]

A need to dominate and be admired can hide beneath the appearance of goodness and generosity. Gaston Pietri wrote:

> If someone is attached to money, he generally knows it and tries to hide it. When an individual is possessed by the need for sensual pleasure, he is conscious of his impulses and he covers them with different behaviors. But, when he is driven by the desire to dominate, it suffices for him to use his very noble gifts in order to satisfy himself. In this way, devotion and zeal sometimes have a frantic race towards power sheltered beneath their mantle.[27]

I like meeting people who accept themselves; I am not speaking about vain persons, but those who are reconciled with their limits and their fragility. Their life is not always easy; they are sometimes judged to be naïve; they know their sufferings and their failures. Those who have accepted themselves are conscious of their errors; they acknowledge them without blaming others; they admit them without resentment and even with a certain sense of humor. These people know how to love their neighbor because they know how to love themselves; they are capable of mercy, the kind that liberates and invites to go beyond. They are people of goodness who accept themselves as imperfect.

Give Us a King

When we refuse to accept ourselves, we often have the tendency to *propel* ourselves toward someone with the image of a strong personality who gives us the impression that I am somebody since there is a powerful and almost perfect individual at the helm.

---

[26] Adrian van Kaam, CSSp., *Religion and Personality* (Englewood Cliffs, NJ: Prentice-Hall, Inc., 1964; Image Books, 1968), 183-184. Paraphrased by the author. —Ed.

[27] Gaston Pietri, *L'heure du choix* (Paris: Desclée de Brouwer, 1989), 147.

We often have the need to idealize someone, to make him a *god* marching in front, who can generate in us dependency and immaturity. "Give us a king who walks before us," said the people of Israel to their God.

Why do so many young people direct themselves toward religious sects? In the absence of a family environment and a paternal authority, they easily turn toward the false security of deceptive fathers and certainties that give/offer protection.

Henri Samson writes:

> How to resist a compassionate and encouraging word? How to reject someone who surrounds us with affection, kindness and protection, and whose prestige as a strong individual satisfies our childish expectations? With reassurance, these emotional ties become more and more invasive. We discover in ourselves a new personality at the service of this individual.
>
> We have encountered a false father. This false father can have different faces. He can be a man who always answers our questions. When we rebel, he speaks vigorously about rebellion; when we are well disposed, he speaks strongly of our needs, understands what is happening in ourselves and expresses it with authority. This false father seems to know everything. He displays so much ease that we think of him as a strong man, an altruistic individual. With time, however, this dependency can become unhealthy. It engenders a different necessity, that which relinquishes responsibility. This dependency increases further when the father imposes himself through continual attention. Without realizing it, we idealize an image and we are guided by our emotional needs.[28]

[28] Henri Samson, *Propos spirituels d'un psychiatre* (Montréal: Bellarmin), 37; Henri Samson/ Paul Garvin, trans. *Spiritual Insights of a Practicing Psychiatrist* (New York: Alba House, 1966).

The Paternalistic Leader

There is an abyss between paternity and paternalism. In their volume, *Seasons of Strength*, Evelyn and James Whitehead explain paternalism:

> The paternalist wants to use his resources for the so-called wellbeing of the group, but with the condition that *his* idea is accepted by the group and his is the best. It is clear, however, that in groups where the leader is paternalistic, that group needs a strong leader. Often, this leader is considered the only one who can lead. He also needs the members of his group to reinforce his image of superiority and power.
>
> With a paternalistic leader, all movement to personal freedom and independence within the group is considered ingratitude (what more do you need than me?) or treason (after all I did for you.) The leader can accomplish much for his group but, at the same time, requires an unbroken dependency towards himself. The paternalistic leader would like to say: "You need me to take care of you and, in return, I need your admiration." The paternalistic leader confuses affection with control. He promises affection in order to control, but does not encourage real growth which brings an individual to become autonomous. The paternalistic leader needs disciples who remain his dependents.[29]

The paternalistic leader often suffers from narcissism and remains a prisoner of his persona. Karen Horney says:

> It provides him with unending confidence that appears enviable to the weak who lack self-confidence. He does not doubt his self-confidence, as he believes that he has

[29] Evelyn Eaton Whitehead, James Whitehead, *Seasons of Strength: New Visions of Adult Christian Maturing* (Garden city, NY: Doubleday, 1984).

a mission, that he is the benefactor to others, that he is generously merciful. He is convinced of his own greatness and his exceptional qualities. He always attempts to confirm this perception of himself by seeking admiration and devotion. This feeling comes from the belief that he can succeed in everything, can control, can seduce and dominate anyone in any situation. In his projects and activities, he cultivates and honors everything that leads him to control. His ability as an organizer is often uncommon. Such an individual needs to dominate lest he is completely lost and powerless.[30]

Accepting Our Shadow with Humor

Accepting ourselves is a long journey. One must first accept this part of our *shadow*, this desire for power that Jung speaks of, this hidden violence, this aggressiveness repressed beneath gentleness, this jealousy that cannot be admitted for fear of having to face it. Accepting ourselves with our poverty, accepting our character defects, accepting to lose face, accepting to be fragile and sinful, is never easy. Accepting reality as it is, without falling into passivity, discouragement, or revolt, is often the first act of humility that leads us on the journey toward serenity.

The second act of humility that brings us reconciliation with ourselves, together with some wisdom, is a sense of humor which is to not take ourselves too seriously.

Thérèse of the Child Jesus was filled with humor toward herself and even knew how to make fun of her faults. Would this not be the beginning of humility? Have we noticed how the proud take themselves so seriously?

[30] Karen Horney, *Neurosis and Human Growth* (New York: Norton, 1950).

In my opinion, true humility starts with self-acceptance mixed with a certain sense of humor. In *La Prière est une fête,* Father A. Lassus said:

> One withdraws into self and closes up to love. In the end, it is a lack of serenity toward oneself, it is living in a type of disgust that feels loathsome and makes one believe that God himself is ready to do the same. What a mistake!
>
> It is a difficult skill to laugh at oneself and accept that God laughs with us. A difficult skill can only be acquired a little at a time with much truth and humility.
>
> What life has taught me is that there is no *great* man on earth, nor any superman, and that the saints have been, are, and will always be limited individuals, unstable, not confirmed with grace in the womb of their mother, nor individuals beyond reproach.
>
> Life has revealed to me (a joyful revelation) that every man is a deeply wounded being...It is the famous concupiscence spoken of in the first letter of Saint John (1 Jn 2:16). One does not live long before discovering this concupiscence in ourselves and others, in our intellect, our will, our heart, and our flesh.
>
> In spite of everything, not becoming angry toward ourselves or others, but believing in the faithful and crazy love of this God who came to save what was lost, who gave sight to the blind and liberty to prisoners, is a wonderful grace.
>
> It is truly a blessed hour in our life when we finally accept ourselves, when we remove our bonds, when we start laughing at ourselves and others like a child, and know that

God laughs with us. It is an excellent lesson about things, age, and grace. It is the beginning of wisdom. [31]

Unveiling Ourselves

Accepting to be ourselves with a certain transparency is a difficult conquest. In his book, *Le Moi transparent*, the psychologist Sydney Jourard clarifies some questions regarding self-discovery. His greatest discernment is that, in the depths of their being, a human has an intrinsic need to uncover oneself, a need to be true and transparent, but, too often, this tendency has been blocked in childhood. The person lives a persona or hides behind a function. The emotions are frozen, the heart is restrained, the body is stiff, and the soul is a prisoner, which often causes serious psychological problems. Jourard writes: "I was asking myself if there was not some link between the refusal of my patients to open themselves up and be recognized by others as they are, and their need to consult a therapist." He arrived at a double conclusion: the constant mask and dissimulation with repression and refusal of the truth can lead to depression and disintegration of the personality; but truth, transparency, openness of the heart and honesty with one's faults and hidden wounds, can literally be a vaccine against emotional illnesses, depressions, and even certain physical diseases.

Being Truthful

Accepting to be ourselves, accepting to be truthful, requires a death to our illusions of grandiosity. The majority of people are not interested in who they are but in the way they are perceived, and the more they lack self-confidence, the more they need to be well perceived by important and influential persons. In our society, people often press onward to the pursuit of appearances or *making a good impression*. Accepting ourselves

[31] Louis-Albert Lassus, *La prière est une fête* (Paris: Éditions du Cerf, 1978). —Ed.

as we are requires a turnaround, a true conversion. The more we age, the more we need to arrive at this reconciliation with ourselves and our limits. We must accept that we will never be approved by all. We must even accept the fact that we desire to be humble but are incapable of it, must accept not having the purity that we would like. We need to accept the fact that the march toward wisdom and maturity is very slow; we need to accept our condition as sinners: doing what one does not want and incapable of doing what one desires. Accepting without passivity, this is the most difficult.

The long journey toward serenity must pass through self-acceptance with a sense of humor. In reality, being transparent and accepting ourselves in our poverty is often the first step toward wisdom and peace of heart.

I Wish to Speak to You

I wish to speak to you with my heart as a child
As we speak sometimes when the lilacs are white
Speak to you of my life and my wounds
I wish to speak to you like the whispering wind

Speak to you about those already gone
To the house in the distance where my father awaits me
I wish to speak to you of what was not said
I wish to speak to you of what was not aging

I wish to speak to you about this adolescent
Who I once was and still am at times
I wish to speak to you of these eyes pure and large
When love was mirrored like a beautiful diamond

I wish to speak to you before I go
But how do I speak when my heart is bleeding
I would like to speak to you a little more about my life
Tell you about my mother and the streets of Saint-Henri

I wish to speak to you before death comes
That you can drink the water flowing from my heart
I would like to speak to you on this spring evening
That I can finally exist as I really am

CHAPTER FOUR

ACCEPTING TO CHOOSE LIFE

Choose life
that you may live.
Deuteronomy 30:19

"God looked at everything he had made and found it very good." This judgement on the world from God should challenge us. At times, what man or woman did not pose the question: Is life worth living? Is the world beautiful? Is life a gift or only adversity?

Let us not forget that, in biblical thought, God reveals himself *within life* throughout human history. For the Hebrews, faith meant opening themselves to the God of life revealed through their history. God called them to walk, to have confidence, to march forward in faith and trust. In faith, Abraham left without knowing his destination, but trusting this God who called him forward. Through faith, Moses left the security of Egypt for the insecurity of the desert, trusting that a life was waiting for him and his people, provided they walked in faith and confidence. The Hebraic faith, the biblical faith, is centered first on *life* and not the afterlife. The world is declared good and very good. Biblical theology, biblical faith, is oriented toward life and not against life. This faith tells us that God is found in life, but this God of life is more than life.

Genesis, the account of creation, clearly affirms the greatness and beauty of life. Material things are delightful and good but one needs to know how to use them. Life is beautiful, life is good and should be appreciated. The world is permeated with God's love.

For the people of the Bible, to be spiritual meant to be *alive* for God and *alive* for the world. It did not signify being *pious* or detached from the world in the sense of disdain for the world or rejection of human life. The Hebrews were so devoted to living life in this world that they had little thought of life after death. It did not mean that they were disbelieving of life after death. But, for them, it was most important to exercise their faith in the present, in *this life*. Death was natural. After living, one accepted to die, but possibly very old and in serenity, "filled with days," as mentioned in the Bible.

The God of the Bible is a God of life who assures us that all he created "is very good."

The God of Life

Do we love life? "When I search for you, my God, I search for a radiant life," wrote St. Augustine. God is delightful, God is joy, God is truly the God of life, the *living* God. The injunction, "You will rejoice before your God, the Lord," is at the heart of the Hebraic tradition. In Hebrew, joy is said *gool*, meaning "to spin under the influence of a violent emotion." In the New Testament, Jesus told his disciples that they *must* live in joy: "I have told you this so that my joy might be in you and your joy might be complete" (Jn 15:11). It is because God is Love, Life, and Joy, and love by nature tends to diffuse itself, for "God created the world so that all creatures would be supplied with his blessings and rejoice in the splendor of his glory."[32] "The God of my joy and my delight," is the title given to God in Psalm 43:4. Therefore it is time to proclaim with courage this *joyful news* of the fullness of life, this *good news* that God is life and

[32] Roman Missal, Eucharistic Prayer IV.

beatitude; that it is beatitude and not suffering, deprivation, and the cross that will have the last word. For humanity has ended up enclosing itself in the false conviction that it must choose between God and life, between God and happiness.

Permission to Live

Life is a gift from God. King Hezekiah cried out: "Those live whom the Lord protects; yours is the life of my spirit...You have given me health and restored my life!...The living, the living give you thanks, as I do today" (Is 38:16, 19). And in the book of Proverbs: "Hear, my son, and receive my words, and the years of your life shall be many" (Prv 4:10).

A psychotherapist has said: "God loves life; he invented it!" Yes, God loves life and he wants us to love it. In a book that makes this known, Paul Tournier described his encounter with a believer who had false education:

> A patient told me one day: "I don't think that this thing is permissible by God because it gives me desires." Such a deformation is generally the result of a negative education. One of my patients, a victim of such an education, once cried out: "I realize that the basic principle received from my parents is this: to abstain from enjoying life. It was not expressly formulated but I am tied up and imprisoned in it." I still think of the young lady, at the door of my office after one of our discussions, to whom I said: "Permission to live." She had mentioned that she set a sort of padlock on life, fearing that, if long repressed, an explosion would burst uncontrollably. She was afraid to live.[33]

[33] Paul Tournier, *Bible et médecine* (Neuchâtel: De la Chaux et Niestlé, 1951); Paul Tournier, trans. Edwin Hudson, *A Doctor's Casebook in the Light of the Bible* (London: SCM press, 1954).

From Our Mother's Womb

In Deuteronomy, we can read the following passage: "Here, then, I have set before you life and prosperity, death and doom...I have set before you life and death, the blessing and the curse. Choose life, then, that you and your descendants may live" (Dt 30:15, 19). Therefore, we must *choose life* in order to love life. Some people choose death and their personality feels its effect. They are not journeying toward serenity but toward a sadness that increases with age and brings them the desire of dying in order to finally relieve them of their life.

In his book on healing wounds beginning from a mother's womb, Nelly Astelli Hidalgo writes the following:

> From the moment of conception in our mother's womb, we are confronted with the antinomy life-death. From the moment we choose death, we enslave our freedom and become beings who are egoistic, timid, frustrated, depressed and envious; we hide behind these defenses built to protect ourselves against others. [34]

Some current studies tend to demonstrate that a child can refuse life from the womb. Others, feeling rejected by their mother, can also refuse it.

According to Astelli Hidalgo:

> Children who do not feel accepted have a poor image of themselves, can appear to be good students, quiet, and amiable, all to obtain love from their parents; however, inside of themselves, they are perturbed by an overwhelming sense of defeat as being unable to face life events. If this rejection has been very significant, these individuals can face depression, a depression that can lead to devastation through drugs, alcoholism or suicide.

[34] Nelly-Astelli-Hidalgo, *Le fruit de tes entrailles: la guérison des blessures reçues dans le sein maternel* (Paris, Fribourg: Éd. Saint-Paul, 1993).

These children fight against life, in fact, against God – the source of life. "I did not ask to live," they often say. In his volume, *Le tout-petit*, Luc Lannoye wrote the following regarding certain children from birth:

> The attitude of some children could be expressed: "Since I don't feel loved, I will try not to depend on those who do not love me, I will depend only on myself." It is a form of egocentric withdrawal; it is a refusal of the condition of a creature loved by God and made to love, a refusal of life as a gift from God. This *choice* will not lead to true life. It can lead a person to turn away from God and others. [35]

Is it possible that persons thirty, forty, or sixty years of age would have the need to renew the *yes* to life that they have refused from the beginning, which has caused their whole life to be based on rejection of life and in sadness?

To Indulge in Complaining

In lieu of desiring *life*, certain people indulge in complaining about the misfortune of living, and this can lead to neurosis or, at least, to a neurotic tendency. This *fear* of living is often a characteristic of the neurotic individual who lives poorly and has a sort of yearning toward failure even though it is said: "He has every reason to be happy." Freud noticed this contradiction when he realized the difficulty for individuals in analysis to attain healing, since they had a problem releasing themselves from their misfortune as if, unconsciously, they were unable to love life and be happy. Freud asked himself if the high degree of culture in our modern civilization did not engender an ideal of moral perfection that was too exacting, thereby generating neuroses.

A psychoanalyst, Renaud de Portzamparc, reflects about the *complaints* that certain people have regarding their life:

[35] Luc Lannoye, *Le tout-petit* (Namur: Coll. Fidélité, 1997).

> *Complaining* is the conversation most often heard in a psychoanalyst's office. All the daily miseries that become exhausting are enumerated as if they are slowly working to erode all the energy of the individual. It is a permanent plaintive tonality about his life that can become tyrannical to his surroundings. It is the complaint of the perpetually unsatisfied neurotic individual. Often, he can spend his entire life complaining as if a means of protection against anxiety.
>
> In this tension, there is an attitude that can be qualified as masochistic. Behind this attitude, there is often a repressed sense of guilt that an individual cannot face. Therefore, a neurotic individual may find, in his abhorrence for life, a source of punishment which helps him live with his guilt. The work of analysis is then to offer the person another vision of life, to know that no one can attain perfection, and that each individual carries some evil in himself. This truth, that may be evident, is sometimes very hard for a client that is trying to attain an ideal for himself. Notably, analysis can bring a beginning of recovery when the neurotic individual arrives at the acceptance, with serenity, of this truth about himself. [36]

As I have said previously, we must accept to be human and accept to be imperfect in order to receive and love our life.

Blessed Are You for My Life

It reverberates in me like soft music, this magnificent saying of St. Clare of Assisi at the moment of her death, words that I would like to repeat at my own death: "Blessed are you, my God, for having given me life!" In order to utter such words, one needs to have loved life, to

[36] Renaud De Portzamparc, "La peine de tous les jours," *Évangile aujourd'hui*, No.144 (Paris: Éditions Franciscaines, 1964).

have loved it in spite of trials and sufferings. Those words reconcile us with the other image that we sometimes have made of Christianity and holiness. The neurotic or masochistic image of which we are, at times, prisoners, speaks only of suffering in this poor life so, as a result, we should not love life too much since it is a *valley of tears*, and we should only be waiting for another life.

As he went along, Francis of Assisi would be singing a hymn to Creation, chatting with birds, stroking a wolf, sleeping under the stars, in nature brimmed with flowers, under an Italian sky. Here is a refreshing image of holiness. True holiness is an explosion, a poem, a wonderment, and a jubilation. It tears the *old skins* to allow us to drink from the new and sparkling wine that revives us. St. Teresa of Avila asked her sisters to dance in the hallways of Carmel, speaking to God with total abandon. Once, she answered a sister who told her of a novice who was having visions: "Well, cut her short, feed her some good chicken, and if her visions persist, bring her to me!" And Francis of Assisi undressed, naked as the day he was born, in front of the bishop of Assisi and his own father, with such simplicity and naivety that the people were touched. Then he said: "Now I have a father, Our Father in heaven." He traveled to Rome with his spiritual sons, wandering on the roads and repeating: "The Lord asks me to be a fool in this world." Francis loved life, sang about life, he, the poet of creation. In spite of his defects, his fragility, and the narcissism of his youth, his life is a masterpiece of grace, and he remains the model of a saint who touches our hearts today.

Possessing before Self-Detaching

A Benedictine religious once said:

> Ahead of self-detachment, one needs to possess self-discipline, maturity and, before obedience, the ability to direct one's life. One needs the acceptance of his sexuality and his own body before living in chastity. Without this,

> we would attract to community repressed individuals who are afraid of life, who want to be directed and, fearful of the world, may decide too quickly to leave it. This would not be supernatural, but the contrary.

We need Christians who love life, because without this, the Gospel would not be the Good News that arises in hearts.

In his volume, *L'Expérience dépressive*, Yves Prigent, a psychiatrist, speaks of depressed people who have not accepted life, who do not love life:

> I saw in them the fear of being carried away by desires, the lack of confidence in what is the most profound, the warmest, the most alive in man: to feel. I saw the effort of these human beings who were tense with a desperate energy from their depths, as a counterpoint to pain: their power, their duty, their knowledge, their possession. In this way, the existence of these persons, who ceased to have an adventurous heart, hardened themselves to attain a coldness and a predictable mechanical pattern. In listening to my patients, I perceived, in the depth of my being, that having confidence in what lives in us, that which is the most profound and warm, represents the necessary condition for healthy living. In our inner being, this confidence seems to merit the beautiful name of faith. [37]

What he says is true and I observe it often in meeting with people, when, from a hardened human being, whose heart and soul were hiding behind a wall, one sees life suddenly bursting forth; the rebirth of a child whose tears can finally come pouring out. Then, one is witness to the marvelous birth of a new human being: "My son was dead; he has come back to life."

[37] Yves Prigent, *L'Expérience dépressive: la parole d'un psychiatre* (Paris: Desclée de Brouwer, 1994).

A Burst of Life

After having listened to someone for a long time, I often saw this stunning miracle, a heart of stone becoming a true heart. *Life* was bursting forth like a resurrection, like a hidden spring; something was starting to flow. The light hidden under the bushel basket of a frigid mind was illuminating new clarity about a childhood long past. A childhood sometimes not lived was suddenly lit up on a radiant face. In further describing the difference between individuals with a dead heart and those alive, Yves Prigent explains this resurrection:

> Let us observe individuals who have accepted to live; note that something lives in them. They are animated, alive, they light up from the inside and, naked in their inner self, they are free. The path that they follow is theirs and they can adjust at any moment. In many aspects, this easiness, this flexibility in their orientation, evokes healthy young children, gracious animals, and is a reminder of the models proposed by the Gospel: the small child, the lilies of the field, the birds who do not sow or reap. This brightness of desire, this transparency of heart, this deep aliveness, this bursting of life, this constant display of new gestures, words, and outlook, are signs that life is truly present and at work in the warm vibration of these human beings.

The words of Jesus, mentioning that we must "become like a child," take another connotation for me when I meet persons that I would say are *falsely mature*, meaning too reasonable, too cerebral, too wise. Some psychologists call these the "normosés" as they seem almost *too normal, too logical, too rational*. At first glance, these persons appear to have equilibrium and self-discipline, but their wound is hidden and repressed under their intellect that seems to function like a *computer*. Donald Winnicott, a psychologist, even claims that the problem of these "normals" is that "they do not seem to have any problems." They lack authenticity and spontaneity. They are too wise, too rational.

Let us not forget that, according to St. Teresa of Avila, the persons who are most hindered, and make little progress on the spiritual path, are those who remain too wise, too reasonable. They cannot enter the fourth mansion, says Teresa of Avila, because everything is too perfect; they would need a desire for folly. St. Paul said: "The wisdom of God is foolishness for man" and, "The one who is wise in the world's judgement, may become a fool in order to become wise." Some wise people desire to control everything, including life, and then become prisoners of their false wisdom. They fear being less wise, thus being considered lesser in the world, and especially lesser by authorities. A Francis of Assisi or a Benedict Labre would be considered much less by a community today: one would fear to be thought of as lacking equilibrium. Unfortunately, one might say that perhaps it is better not to become a saint than to be judged insane.

Surging from the Heart

The psychotherapist Yves Prigent wrote:

> I am happy when an adult comes to me tired and subdued, and leaves jumping like a child. I always try to facilitate the melting of ice by which the polar caps start to melt and disappear, irrigated by the warm currents surging from the heart. What I discern from my psychiatric practice is that the troubles arising from the widespread and common word depression are born through the refusal to be who we are.

How many people do not live but only exist as prisoners of their function and persona, prisoners of their "idealized image" that was sometimes dragged along from their youth. They work, even have success in many areas, do many things, but their interior child is dead, buried in the cave of their deepest self. Something in them is dead. In a slip of the tongue, a depressed priest said to a psychologist:

"You see, I came to the cemetery...(Oh! Pardon, to the seminary) at 16 years of age!" Sometimes the words speak *loudly*, and the unconscious reveals itself when depression cracks everything. Many persons seem to *live* but are not yet born. The *liveliness of the heart* has been frozen by the fear of living. These persons are not free internally. Eric Fromm affirmed that the greatest of life's tragedies is that most human beings die before being fully born since they never really lived. To an atheist, who was asking Father Maurice Zundel if there is life after death, he answered: "Undoubtedly, one needs to see if there is life before death." And when he was asked if he believed in God, he answered: "And you, do you believe in man?" He added: "Jesus accepted life. He glorified it. He transfigured it and gave it an infinite dimension so we may live it with wonder and passion." Father Zundel also liked to quote this reflection from a monk: "I have as much devotion to eating my soup as in celebrating Mass." And added: "This word from a monk is admirable because it brings us to discover the sacred side of life and the sacred side of all the gestures of our existence."

As Christians, we must accept, welcome, and love life.

To Welcome Life

Life is filled with feelings. In fear to face them, however, we have killed the life bursting in ourselves. Lytta Basset writes:

> Experience demonstrates that a feeling expelled through a door, returns through a window or, moreover, a feeling dismissed from consciousness hides in the unconscious. Therefore, every feeling is to be acknowledged and confessed before God because, as "negative" as it might be, this feeling carries within it something of life; every feeling responds to, vibrates with, and echoes what is lived. Hence,

> it brings me into relationship with the living God. Every feeling is to be accepted (not repressed) even if it is to ask God in prayer to be delivered from it, because this feeling links me to life, to this living God who desires that I feel my existence in order to live it fully. No feeling can kill a person, others or myself, and certainly not God. On the other hand, repressing or killing a feeling is to kill something alive. When we return to life and our heart overwhelms us, it is sometimes with amazement: "It was so simple!" It is the sign of a renewed accord with the original child who starts to relive in ourselves. One must learn to live again. To live is good even if, at times, it hurts terribly. Living is good.[38]

I will always remember a man close to his thirties from a distant city who, for a long time, repressed his anger toward God because of past events. He was sad, slept poorly and lived with anxiety which, at times, prevented him from working. One day, I told him: "You have a right to be angry at God." I quoted some passages from Job and Jeremiah to him. Something lit up in his eyes. Then, I simply asked him to look at my crucifix and shout his anger. It was as if, by the fury of its waters, a dam suddenly burst open. With cries and rage, he shouted his anger toward God. Then he started to weep softly and, to my surprise, ended with a beautiful prayer to God from the depth of his heart.[39] From that evening on, he began to be transformed and his anxiety disappeared. Through experience, I have lived what Lytta Basset referred to above: "Every feeling is to be acknowledged and confessed before God because any feeling, as "negative" as it might be, carries within it something of life...On the other hand, repressing or killing a feeling is to kill something alive."

[38] Lytta Basset, *La Joie imprenable: pour une théologie de la prodigalité* (Genève: Labor et Fides, 1996), 226.

[39] The person in question has allowed their experience to be shared here.

Living in One's Body

To be alive is to live in one's body and not disdain it. The Bible says: "The sign of a good heart is a cheerful countenance" (Sir 13:25).[40] The body reveals a person since the body is the sign of the soul in a human being. Therefore, modern thinkers consider the face and the expression an epiphany of our interiority, a revelation of our soul. On a face and in the eyes, one can immediately see if a person is alive, if they truly live. Why, for example, does the face of a child move us so much if not that his innocence is not hidden under a mask and, therefore, reveals life to us with all its freshness and spontaneity. Without fear and restraint, through his look and his body, he tells us his wonder, his confusion, his joy or pain, and all this instinctively. To be alive is to feel oneself *living* in one's own body; if I am able to speak of life, it is because I feel it within myself, it is that I am vibrant. Charles de Koninck said:

> The first notion of life, the one that we will always return to, comes first of all from the internal experience of living. To live is to touch, taste, smell, see – to discern these sensations one from another, to imagine, recall, love, hate, move from place to place, to rejoice, be sad, understand, reason, and to will; life is first known in the conscious exercise of these operations.[41]

In fact, in occidental society and the Christian education of the past, one insisted strongly on the spirit, the intellect and the will, what is referred to as the rational objective elements of the human being as opposed to the subjective, affective, and emotional elements. The first was generally considered superior, the other inferior. In fact, one seemed to forget that Jesus Christ lived with all kinds of emotions. He did not fear weeping publicly and did not fear living in anguish, which attests to his tenderness and compassion, and reflects sensitivity and

[40] Sir: 13: 25: The heart changes one's face, either for good or for evil.

[41] Charles de Konink, *Introduction à l'étude de l'âme*, préface au livre de Stanislas Quentin (Québec: Université Laval, 1948), 5.

intuition which remains for us, now close to the third millennium, a brilliant example of a life fully human.

Having a Sense of the Body

When we read the Gospel, we never see an invitation to become a pure spirit, a man or woman pseudo-angelic, that some spiritualities have pretended to portray as Christian. Jesus Christ is not an angel, he is a true man, a man incarnate. In all the pages of the Gospel, one can find a sort of passion, which animates the heart of Jesus, for this *embodied* man with whom he shares his destiny. This God "who became flesh," does not look suspiciously at all flesh. At no time in the Gospels does one see Jesus condemning the joy and pleasure that man encounters in living all the sensible dimensions of his life. St. Paul wrote to his disciples in Corinth: "The body, however, is not for immorality but for the Lord, and the Lord is for the body...therefore, glorify the Lord in your body" (1Cor 6:13, 20). St. Paul does not disdain the body, on the contrary. When a Christian Orthodox philosopher such as Basile Roganov, for example, dares to write: "The atheist is the one who does not have a sense of the body," he is much closer to the Gospel and the apostolic Fathers than the Jansenism that shaped so many Christians of past generations into persons often paralyzed with fear of the body and with obsession about carnal sins. Georges Hourdin wrote that: "Fifty years ago, Christians were saying to all: this earth is a valley of tears. They were claiming to despise the goods of this world...this attitude was often hypocritical. It was a moralism and the worst kind of moralism."[42] Fortunately, the Second Vatican Council brought a Copernican Revolution concerning the attitude that Christians should have toward the world and its values. "The joy and hope, the sadness and anguish of people of this time, particularly the poor and all those who suffer, are also the joy and hope, sadness and anguish of the disciples of Christ. There is nothing truly human that does not echo in

[42] Georges Hourdin, *Dieu en liberté* (Paris: Stock, 1973).

their hearts."[43] This Christian notion: "There is nothing truly human that does not find an echo in our hearts," must be integrated into all the other aspects of the personality. To be an expert in philosophy and theology is insufficient for entering into communication with one's peers.

To Live Is to Feel

Jack Dominian, a Christian psychiatrist, asserts:

> Contemporary Christianity must be conscious that people are in a quest for love, for healing, and for growth far beyond the traditional concepts of service to the body and the spirit. The young in particular will require, in the future, another dimension that can reflect a world of feelings, emotions, and instinct. Christianity is rich with treasures in that sphere, and it is very tragic that centuries of legalism have given birth to an arid affectivity which has virtually atrophied the sense of Christianity.[44]

To live is not only to reason and think, it is also *to feel.* As a psychiatrist, Jack Dominian gives an explanation for the exit of many priests after years of ministry. Often, we can say too quickly (to stop the feeling of guilt) that "it was a lack of prayer" or that the priest was living with serious psychological problems. However, according to Dominian:

> One can assert that the main reason for this exit is a late maturity through which the objectives of the teenage years were attained only after thirty years or sometimes forty or fifty years. It is a phenomenon of the maturation of the personality which does not involve psychological

[43] *L'Église dans le monde de ce temps: constitution pastorale "Gaudium et Spes"* (Montreal: Fides, 1966); Pastoral Constitution on the Church in the Modern World, *"Gaudium et Spes"* (December 7, 1965).

[44] Jack Dominian, *Maturité affective et vie chrétienne* (Paris: Cerf), 152.

> problems in any way. Furthermore, when these men have lived several years in their vocation, the urgent need to leave and live their lives in a different way violently overturns the habits and loyalty that are deeply rooted...In psychological terms, their situation is easily understood. They have themselves the need to live, the need of freedom and personal responsibility. They have never really lived. Clearly, in the future, the formation to the priesthood must uncover all underlying immaturity.

A vocation should not be an escape, a need to be admired, a way to assert oneself, or a fear of the body or sexual feelings. Jack Dominian adds:

> For me, it seems essential that the religious life should not become a refuge for those afraid of their body. What I mean is that men and women who are estranged from their bodies in feelings of affection, anger, or sexual feelings, should not be accepted. It seems to me that the criteria of admission that exclusively insists on the intellectual aspects of the candidates, and ignores their physical and affective maturity, gives a disservice to the ideal of religious life. This ideal needs to attract complete individuals for whom religious life is not an escape into the spiritual nor a substitute for a physical or affective integrity.

Let us be wary of persons who are strangers to their heart and their body, who did not experience a real childhood or teenage years.[45] They have not lived and cannot truly give themselves because they do not possess themselves. "Those who seek religious life because they

[45] "Effortless chastity, especially so frequently seen in emotionally developing young people, is usually a camouflage behind alluring systems of compensation. The subject can be brought to very brilliant social or cultural achievements to escape the counterpart of the sexual delay which is infantilism. On the other hand, poorly developed sexuality is an inevitable testament to poorly sublimated aggressiveness. This can then feed with passion, tendencies towards domination and possession." ("Direction spirituelle et psychologie," *Études carmelitaines* [Bruges: Desclée de Brouwer, 1951]).

cannot bear the normal requirements of society are not in the right place," says Jack Dominian.

One must accept life and love it if we are to become witnesses of God's love in the world.

To Be Moved

One needs "to be moved every day by something or someone in order to become real" according to Bergmann. If we do not accept life, if we repress our heart of a child, we become dried up. Then a sort of interior hardness appears that Reich describes this way: "Under the skin of the body, under the surface of a lively appearance, there emerges a hard shell, inflexible, immobile, obstructed by a *muscular armor*."

The armor would need to be broken and the plating melted. However, this *muscular armor*, this *interior hardness*, yields only through trust that is given to another. One needs to accept being loved, to accept receiving. It is sometimes necessary to convince a person that they are the prisoner of a pledge in their childhood, such as: "I will never cry," "I will save my family," "If I am always strong and serious, I will be admired," or "I will never accept to be loved," etc.

A person can refuse life to protect themselves. To heal, one must be conscious of this dangerous protection, this *childhood* pledge, this interior rigidity. Then, one must allow the shell to slowly fall away, to shatter one's image and, with a naked heart, expose oneself as weak and vulnerable in front of someone who accepts us the way we are. We must give ourselves the right to live, the right to feel and to weep. "Blessed are you who are now weeping, for you will laugh," says the Gospel. One would need to read the Gospel with new eyes. "Young man, I order you, get up!" "The young girl is not dead, she sleeps." "Come out of the tomb!" "Untie him." All the life bursting through these words makes us rise and come out of our tombs. We become a child again, leaping for joy, allowing tears when needed, being moved, and living one day at a time because "sufficient for a day is its own troubles," and "why worry," because "the Father himself loves you." The wedding at Cana, the wine that overflows and is "much better than the first wine," those children who are kissed and blessed because "it is to these that the Kingdom belongs," the anger that explodes, the cracking whip that overturns the tables, the displayed anguish that expresses sadness and the need for others: "My soul is sad even unto death. Stay here and watch with me." What a life! A life expressed with outbursts, with cries and jubilation, with true tears and true joy! This Jesus is so different than the chief priests and the Pharisees hidden behind their shells and their personas, too strained and too rigid.

Cutting the Ties

The God of the Bible is the God of Life who desires that a person becomes themselves and lives. On this topic, there is an eloquent passage in the Bible. It is undoubtedly not without reason that Luke, a doctor, reports it:

> Each year his parents went to Jerusalem for the feast of Passover, and when he was twelve years old, they went up according to festival custom. After they had completed its days, as they were returning, the boy Jesus remained behind in Jerusalem, but his parents did not know it. Thinking that he was in the caravan, they journeyed for a day and looked for him among their relatives and acquaintances, but not finding him, they returned to Jerusalem to look for him. After three days they found him in the temple, sitting in the midst of the teachers, listening to them and asking them questions, and all who heard him were astounded at his understanding and his answers. When his parents saw him, they were astonished, and his mother said to him, "Son, why have you done this to us? Your father and I have been looking for you with great anxiety. And he said to them, "Why were you looking for me? Did you not know that I

must be in my Father's house? But they did not understand what he said to them (Lk 2:41-50).

Jesus was twelve years old; he had accompanied his parents to Jerusalem, but instead of returning with them, he remained behind in the temple conversing with theologians. Naturally his mother rebuked him when she found him. This Jesus, a teenager, fled for three days, cut ties with Mary and Joseph, and pursued the sense of his own mission. He answered his mother without guilt but firmly: "Did you not know that I must be in my Father's house?" As with all mothers who often have difficulty cutting the tie with their child, especially their son, Mary is *anguished.* "Your father and I have been looking for you with great anxiety," she said. At twelve years old, Jesus did what some young people of today, even at twenty-five years of age, have not succeeded in accomplishing. At twelve years old, he started to detach from his mother to become himself; he was not destined to be only what his mother imagined or wanted, but what God, his Father, called him to be, even if it grieved his mother. In the Bible, there are examples of maternal domination, of the "mother complex" as mentioned by some psychologists. We can quote this passage in the Gospel where we see the mother of two disciples, James and John, who had ambition for her sons. She approached Jesus and asked him: "Command that these two sons of mine sit, one at your right and the other at your left" (Mt 20:20-21). Here, there is the naive projection of an ambitious mother regarding her sons that we can often observe, and that can even prevent a son from being faithful to his true mission.

We all know that, in order to become a mature adult, one day we must *leave* our parents without feeling guilty because our life is *different* than theirs, and our personal mission is the most important.

Losing One's Life to Find It

One must lose his life to find it. "Whoever loses his life (his former life) finds it." It is a question of losing that *dependent* life, which was not a life, a dead-alive life; we need to die to our *false-self* in order to recover our true self, because often, as mentioned by a therapist: "We sometimes live a mechanical life which is carried out under a protective *false-self* that suffocates the *true-self*, a creature with desires, the child in the depths of our heart." Life is not programmed, nor mechanical, nor decided in advance. Life is a surprise of leaps, laughs, cries, successes, defeats, and a wounded heart. Life is "dancing feet" and "music to the ear," as sung by Gilles Vigneault. How many people have accepted life, their own life? How many have truly said *yes* to life and can say like St. Clare of Assisi: "Be blessed my God, for having given me life!"? Some people are already dead before dying. Like the older son in the parable of the father and his two sons, they never really lived. The good, the serious, the faithful son never "celebrated with his friends." Every day he fulfilled his duty, seriously, meticulously, working in the fields even during a celebration. This older son, faithful and serious, who never has time for entertainment, does not truly live. He is the model son of the family, a son that many parents would dream of having, who tries to respond to the demands of his "idealized image" as a good and perfect young man. When he hears singing, music, and dancing, he fumes interiorly and cannot tolerate it, because it is too *lively*, too spontaneous, too joyful, too undoubtedly childlike for him, a man of principle and duty, who "works for his father all these years" but never truly met him within the framework of the heart and affectivity. This older son thinks himself alive, but he is dead inside. The prodigal younger son was dead but *lives* again. He is *alive* and can joyously dance on his return to the paternal home and celebrate the loving tenderness of his father. In another chapter, we will return to this parable, but it was the idea here to begin a reflection on this older son who does not live, who appears to distaste life, who is not truly living. But the prodigal son who left his parents' house recognizes himself as a sinner, as weak, and meets his father heart to heart which leads him back to life and the experience of mercy and forgiveness.

The Process of Separation

In order to live, one needs the courage to become oneself, one needs to *leave* home, a family, a mentality. To be true to one's personal vocation, one needs to leave like Abraham, who "left" without knowing where he was to go, like Jacob who "fought all night with a stranger" and was wounded at the hip, and like so many others, sometimes misunderstood by their family, when they decide to be faithful to their personal vocation. Some words in the Gospel appear to be harsh when we pay little attention to their meaning. Jesus said: "If anyone comes to me without hating his father and mother, wife and children, brothers and sisters, and even his own life, he cannot be my disciple" (Lk 14:21). I think that the word "hate" used by Jesus in this text could mean "a process of separation." Jesus also came to bring the *sword*, to *separate*, to *cut* what was too *fusional*. In fact, I cannot become the person that I am called to be if I do not, in a certain way, *separate* myself from my family and, often, from my disincarnate ideal. This ideal is, at times, a simple *projection* of the "idealized image" that others have fabricated about me and that can oblige me to display a persona that is not truly myself inside. How many individuals – sometimes late in their forties – remain *dependent* on what their parents and family think of them. They become incapable of making a decision that would grieve their loved ones and thereby tarnish their "image." When Jesus speaks of *hate*, in this sense, he means to have enough freedom to *cut the ties that are too deeply rooted* which can prevent me from going forward toward the life that God offers me, therefore not responding to my true personal vocation. This would cause me to shatter my "idealized image" and separate from family members who, not understanding well enough, would suffer a profound grief. Jesus said to someone who wanted to follow him but was too attached to his father: "Let the dead bury the dead...you, follow me." To follow Him is to become what we are called to be, that unique vocation that no one can *carry out* in my place. This is *living* and loving life because it is "my" life and not another's life that other people enticed me to live for my so-called good.

Live and Tell

We are afraid to live and, at times, even to love life. Some Christians can falsely think that loving life does not appear spiritual enough and one would almost need to disdain joy, pleasure, livelihood. Life is replete with emotions: negative and positive feelings. This is living. So many wounds remain repressed and hidden. Sometimes one thinks that these will disappear by keeping silent. Well, they *do not disappear*, and will emerge in a *different* way through what is known as psychosomatic illnesses, anguish, apparent frigidity, etc. A Christian therapist, Jean François Noble, expresses it this way:

> In therapy, there is often a false fear that my situation will worsen if I speak of my ills, my wounds. In reality, I would simply be getting in touch with repressed emotions buried for a long time. These emotions long repressed, felt intensely, but not expressed, make the situation worse. Keeping silence heightens the problem; speaking with a trusted person brings, at first, emotional turmoil but, afterward, the situation is examined more calmly. When we enter into what we seek to avoid and revive it, the movement of liberation occurs; one starts the process of healing.
>
> It is the movement of Christ himself. He entered into death. In his interior, he experienced fear, sadness, and anguish. From within, he generated a transformation, converting death into resurrection. In the therapeutic and emotional sphere, when I enter into my sufferings, my fears, my anguish, my sadness, or my anger, not alone but accompanied by someone else, I live again in expressing these, and can start seeing things in a different way.[46]

[46] Jean François Noble, *Oser être soi-même,* [ch. Chapons des-Prés 4] Radio Reveil-Paroles de vie, 1995.

When One Does Not Live

What happens when we do not live? We become tense like the "older son" of the parable, we are consumed by our duty, but without joy, and become jealous of these "prodigal sons" who come from afar but are transformed by Forgiveness. We then take refuge behind rules and principles which are often only human precepts and provide a false security. Frustrated and discouraged by the high standard we have pursued, we are interiorly irritated (at best consciously, or at worst, unconsciously) with ourselves, with others and, sometimes, with God. We live in a sort of existential *emptiness* that we find difficult to understand, and we tend to fill this emptiness in many different ways.

Human Beings Who Live

In your life, you may recall persons you remember with feelings of gratitude and peace. It could be an old grandmother, an uncle, a religious, a father, a priest...whoever. But on further reflection, you may recall that all these persons were *alive*, that in them was a quality of *life*, a transparency, a flexibility. Leo Buscaglia describes them:

> These persons recognize their psychological and physical need for intimacy, a need to connect with others at a deep and significant level. They accept their life. These mature life-artists are spontaneous, welcoming, adjustable, and receptive to new experiences. They respect people and the society they live in, even when they disagree with them. These mature individuals have a deep sense of spirituality and live with an awe of life's gifts. They have a flexible and non-conformist sense of identity.[47]

In fact, often these individuals do not appear *perfect* or without *faults*, but they are essentially *alive*. J. Stone said: "The truly mature adult is the one who emerges from childhood without losing the

[47] Leo F. Buscaglia, *La personnalité* (Montreal: Éd. Le Jour, 1984).

best characteristics of childhood. He retains his fundamental emotional strength."

Sometimes, parents tell their sons and daughters that "it is amazing how serious they are for their age." Do they realize that it can be a "false maturity," and a neurotic wound?

Too Perfect

In *The Drama of the Gifted Child,* Alice Miller explains the hidden wound of the model child, too perfect, who was idealized by his parents, and at thirty, forty, or fifty years of age, finds himself *alone* and *lost* behind his image. There is here something profoundly tragic and moving, when a person in need of help literally panics and has enormous difficulty admitting to themselves the need for therapy. Ironically, they prefer to attack those who would like to help. Starting therapy would signify that they are not perfect, and their childhood was not ideal. On the contrary, they need to admit that, at times, they were not truly a child. But the anxiety can be so strong that this person would do anything to prevent such a humiliating admission of needing help, because asking for help would also mean to admit being wounded and, perhaps, more wounded than others. When this person, man or woman, can remove their mask and, for the first time, express the rage and pain of not having really lived, and to have become an *adult* too quickly, then there is hope of healing. For these individuals, the great difficulty is to stop rationalizing and repressing their heart of a wounded child. As long as emotions – pain, anger, and sadness – remain hidden and repressed, and a person refuses to express these feelings by showing vulnerability and fragility in front of someone, this person will continue to construct an "idealized image." They will run, exhausting themselves, to prove that they are a great or special person who needs admiration in order to live. This person does not live; they are interiorly dead with a strained smile. Their look is not luminous. It is sad and gloomy because there is a great emptiness existing in their heart from a long-ago childhood. There is a little child who weeps at length within this adult who appears so rational.

Feeding Our Heart

To live is "to let ourselves be moved each day by something or someone." I say explicitly *to be moved* and not only to accomplish endeavors that can assure admiration and affection from others. Receiving from others and being moved is often most difficult for our pride and our unconscious narcissism.

To live is letting oneself be loved. True love often seems difficult because of our intrinsic egoism, but it creates more growth than any other experience. It develops maturity in the heart, soul, and our entire being. To truly live is to know how to love and also to accept being loved. I am touched by a phrase often recited by Jean Gabin on the radio: "A day when someone loves you is a beautiful day." I would say: "It is a very beautiful day." To live is to love and let oneself be loved.

Yves Prigent says:

> May we not be deprived of this nourishment and this breath. Let us utilize and profit from these signs of life provided by other humans, our brothers, in pleasure and in death. Let us use and benefit from the feelings that seize us in reading Rimbaud, in singing Vigneault, in listening to Bach, in drinking a glass of wine, in contemplating the sea caressing the face of the rocks. Let us acknowledge that the world never speaks of anything significant if we only seek to analyze it. We need to live life.

A True Christian Spirituality

One day a question was asked of a Christian, Lawrence Richards, in what does a true incarnate Christian spirituality of life consist. He answered: "A Christian spirituality is simply to live one's life in the world of today in union with God."[48]

In fact, our model should be Jesus himself who lived among people, with them – empathizing, smiling and weeping with them – open, loving, welcoming, proclaiming the truth without fear, but also respecting each person. He was in the world but always in union with the Father, spending time alone with Him in prayer and then returning to the people, "eating at the table of sinners," inviting himself to Zacchaeus' home, a thief and a tax collector: "Come down, I must stay at your house." Jesus was unified, transparent, always able to love the sinner while rejecting sin.

I sincerely believe that a Christian spirituality begins through friendship with the God incarnate, the *Holy Humanity of Jesus*, with his human heart beating in his resurrected body. St. Teresa of Avila said: "Prayer is an interchange of friendship in a heart-to-heart exchange." In fact, a Christian spirituality needs two components: first, "alone with the Friend in silence or in exchange" – this is the aspect of a *personal prayer of adoration, solitude with God*; and "with the Friend, present to friends" – *engagement with others*, presence in friendship, this God whom we meet in the hearts of others. Sometimes adults and young people need to meet God through our presence to them before they encounter a personal experience of a heart-to-heart with the Father. "You are Christ's Body, what have you done with Him?" as John Littleton has sung.

I would say that *intimacy* with God, in a true spirituality that is not an avoidance of the world, but a meeting person-to-person, brings us gently to a capacity of intimacy with others. When we feel loved by God, when we have recognized ourselves as weak, poor but forgiven, we have less fear of being discovered by others.

---

[48] Lawrence O. Richards, *A Practical Theology of Spirituality* (Grand Rapids: Zandervan, 1987).

One can observe that, even in prayer at times, some people are not themselves; their prayer is impersonal. How strange!

I believe, says James Houston, that it reflects a fear of intimacy, a fear of opening up and revealing ourselves as we are. Even with God, we hide our true feelings. All this is, in part, due to the fact that we have very few friends with whom to share, not only our ideas, but also our emotions, our joys and our sufferings. Could it not be the reason that we seek more "to perform" than "to be" and "to live"?

It Is Very Good

To love life is to expand the cry of Genesis: "Yes, it is very good," and to believe that, in spite of everything, it is worthwhile to live. Loving life is to see, with lit up eyes of the heart, like Jesus who was looking at "the birds of the sky, the lilies of the field, the sunsets," and to be filled with wonder even though he knew "what is in the human heart." Loving life is praying with a heart of flesh to the God who came in the flesh with a human Heart – this God who loved people so much, who loves them now, and who asks for confidence, abandonment, forgiveness, and to love through heartbreaks and sufferings.

Loving life is accepting little by little to have a heart of flesh, a natural heart, and to thank God for this gift.

The Flesh Will Be So Beautiful

We will rise you see in the freshness of dawn
The tears on our cheeks will be flowers
We will recognize ourselves and no longer be afraid
Over our cold bodies will flow warm water

It will be beautiful you see like an apple tree in bloom
Like the eyes of a child at the dawn of happiness
Our hearts will be agile like our youth
Eternity will be born in the fire of tenderness

No more death no more pain no more tears nor fears
But laughter as fresh as the perfume of childhood
Our bodies will be able to dance with beauty and confidence
Purity of heart will invade our senses

The flesh will be so beautiful and our beautiful faces
Will be so transparent as to reveal our souls
And the sweetness of loving will be like a stream
Where our lives will plunge like a trembling child

The future will become youth once again
Like a beautiful month of May of eternal tenderness
We will recognize ourselves and no longer be afraid
The tears on our cheeks will be flowers

CHAPTER FIVE

ACCEPTING TO RECOGNIZE ONESELF AS A SINNER

I did not come to call the just,
but the sinner.

Jesus Christ

The saints are not at all what we think or imagine them to be. Some humanist American psychologists noticed that we have not taken seriously the assertions of most saints about the multiplicity of their weaknesses. One thought that they pretend to recognize themselves as sinners, another thought they express excessive scruples or false modesty. "Reality is altogether different," affirms the psychotherapist Yves Prigent. "One does not live passionately and deeply from the heart without facing limitations and weaknesses at every moment, without multiplying conflicts, slips and mistakes. Natural virtue is for the strong, the adult, the powerful, the religious, and not for the weak, the children, and the saints."[49] The saints are not the *virtuous* in a moral sense, they are not even the strong-willed or heroes, they are, first of all, lovers who, in their weaknesses, confess their faults without false culpability. "I feel a great joy," said St. Thérèse of the Child Jesus, "to know that I am imperfect, and to feel it in myself, and to need mercy."

[49] Prigent, *L'expérience dépressive.*

We Are Blind

After accepting our basic humanity and imperfections, we need to go a step further and accept ourselves as sinners. In order to recover our heart of flesh on this long journey toward the serenity of mature aging and the rediscovery of our heart of a child, there is a necessary passage by which we need to accept taking off our mask, accept the condition of a sinner, and even accept this unconscious pharisaism that often lives in ourselves, whether man or woman, Christian, priest, or religious.

Why is the question of Pharisees often brought up in the Gospel? Does the Word of God simply mean that this issue only existed two thousand years ago at the time of Jesus? If we read the Word of God, not only for *those times*, but mostly for *these times*, is it possible that we need to look in the mirror for the Pharisee persona? Is it possible that an unconscious Pharisee hides in each of us? Let us not forget that the Pharisees were people like us.

We always have a certain degree of pharisaism in us. In the Gospel, Jesus called them hypocrites, liars, serpents, murderers, and white sepulchers. It is difficult to admit that we can become one of them but...there is in us the original wound that causes us to hide behind our persona, to seek power and domination, to elevate ourselves above others and desire to be *the embodiment of Moses*, although not to serve, but to be admired. We, like the Pharisees, can become "blind" (Mt 23:16-17, 19, 24-26), "serpents" (Mt 23:33), "nest of vipers" (Mt 3:7, 12:34, 23:33), and even "liars and hypocrites."

Behind the Image...Emptiness

I am distressed at times in seeing that many individuals are not making efforts *to be someone* but seeking to be *valued for something*; they do not desire to fill their soul or feed their heart, but desire to occupy a *position*, do not ask themselves how they are clothed inside but, rather, what suit, what mask to wear. An artistic photographer, who has photographed several well-known personalities, shared with me:

> When one takes the time to look into the mystery of a person, a true photo is sometimes terrible in its truth, and even worse is that the photographed person does not realize it, so attached are they to their persona. When one photographs faces for a long time, one can read behind the plastic smile the fear and the mask behind the appearance of dignity. One can see eyes that want to be gentle but betray a terrible violence behind their look. One sees people recognized as benefactors and charitable, but their face reflects a stiffness in order to hide, at all cost, a terrific fear of being discovered behind their apparent strength and dignity.

This confidential statement of the photographer reminds me of what has been repeated many times: "Your words can lie but never your body." Oscar Wilde wrote something remarkable: "A man who aspires to become someone who is not himself – congressman, wealthy trader, pastor, judge or famous lawyer, or anything else – will always succeed. And that is his punishment. Whoever seeks after a mask ends up living through a mask." So many people repress their heart and hide their wounds in order to become a *persona*. The beginning of true humility and healing from our pharisaism is to notice our pride. It is a tremendous light to begin seeing that even our generosity and desire to be good are mixed with a pharisaic pride.

Suppressing Our Conscience

Scott Peck, a psychotherapist and author of the world best seller, *The Road Less Travelled*, writes this in his admirable and clearly understood book on evil:

> These people do not believe themselves evil; on the contrary, they see much evil in others. As they consider themselves

> above all reproach, they are irritated by those who reproach them. They sacrifice others to preserve their own image of perfection. Concerned about protecting their image of perfection, they constantly seek to maintain the appearance of moral purity. It is a great preoccupation of theirs. They are really sensitive to the opinion of others. They are often well dressed, punctual at work and their life is flowing without any rebuke. The words *image*, *appearance*, and *exteriorly*, are crucial to understand them. Even as they do not have much desire to be good, bad people have an intense desire to appear good. Their *goodness* is only an ostentation. This is why I call them *people of the lie*. It sometimes happens that one can recognize evil behind the disguise. We see the smile that hides hate, the smart and soft expression that hides fury, the velvet under the iron hand. People of the lie are such disguise experts that it is sometimes difficult to recognize their evil. Their disguise is often impenetrable. They work hard and exhaust themselves in their sustained effort to project the image of their honorability. There is only one grief they cannot endure: the sadness in discovering their own sins and imperfections. These persons are lost when seeking a psychotherapist because they do everything to avoid the dreadful trial of an examination of conscience.[50]

In this text of a psychotherapist, we have a perfect mirror of *pharisaism*. Jesus says to the Pharisees that they are "blind." It happens that we ourselves can be blind like them. First of all, we are often *blinded* through the *admiration* that people have of us, and by the *esteem* that we subtly seek in order to increase our self-esteem. When I give retreats, I always fear presenting the *image* of a priest without faults, and thus being idealized. This is why I often tell my retreatants that if they lived with me, they would see my defects and my wounds.

[50] M. Scott Peck, *Les gens du mensonge* (Paris: J'ai lu, 1983); M. Scott Peck, *People of the Lie: the Hope for Healing Human Evil* (New York: Simon and Schuster, 1983).

As the proverbs say: "No one is a prophet in his own country" and "There is no great man but his butler." The Pharisees were highly esteemed people, but they were prisoners of their idealized image which led them to hypocrisy and lies.

Secondly, we are, at times *blinded* by our moral principles and we look from on high at the sinners we think have fallen so low. St. Thérèse of the Child Jesus wanted to live with former prostitutes in order to appear like them in the eyes of everyone. This is true holiness. Amidst good Christians of prayer and scripture meetings, who would want to be seen as a thief or prostitute? We are all a bit pharisaic and believe ourselves to be just. Finally, at times, we are blinded by our knowledge and even our intellectual understanding of theology that, without love and without humility, can easily mask our corruption.

Pride and Arrogance

In speaking of pharisaic pride, Scott Peck uses the expression "malignant narcissism." There is a certain normal narcissism such as the desire to succeed, to be proud of oneself in a normal way, but "malignant narcissism" leads to seeking *power* at all cost. According to the author, malignant and abnormal narcissism is characterized by the constant search for power and admiration, an excessive intolerance of being questioned, and foremost, criticism of facts and gestures, a strong preoccupation with one's public image, a presumption of respectability, and the repression of hateful feelings or the desire for vengeance hidden under a smile or generous philanthropic endeavors.

> It is the image that needs to be transmitted because they must not give evidence of weakness or imperfection. Therefore, they must display an appearance of organizing everything, of assuming *responsibility*. Think of the psychological energy needed by these people to continually sustain their false image! How do they live? Basically, they are afraid, they are terrified of the idea that their mask

> could fall, and they would then be exposed to themselves and in the eyes of the whole world. Therefore, they live in constant fear of having to confront their own evil one day.[51]

Jesus said to the Pharisees: "If you at least said: 'We are blind,' I could cure you, but you say: 'We see,' so your sin remains."

The Pharisee: A Wounded Child

Where does this certainty originate which we carry inside, that love needs to be earned, that we have to merit the affection of others through our actions? Does it come from an old wound? We all, more or less, lack some confidence in ourselves, we hide under a false confidence because we fear recognizing our faults and weaknesses. In *The Respectable Addicts*, Barbara Killinger writes:

> However, even if exteriorly he appears sure of himself and independent, inside he has a terrible need of admiration from others in order to live. Under his facade of false confidence, there is in him an eternal fight to resolve the wounds from long ago and the fears of a weak child who has a great need of approval.[52]

In fact, if I do not feel accepted for myself, if I do not feel loved unconditionally for who I am, then I will constantly try to find ways to *assert* myself in my works. Is it not an eternal truth that a human being intensely desires to be accepted as he is? Nothing in this life has a more disastrous effect than the experience of not being loved and accepted for oneself.

The Pharisee is like a child who does not feel accepted. He needs to display his virtues: "The Pharisee took up his position and spoke this prayer to himself, 'O God, I thank you that I am not like the rest of humanity – greedy, dishonest, adulterous, or even like

[51] Ibid.

[52] Barbara Killinger, *Workaholics: the respectable addicts* (Toronto: Key Porter Books, 1991).

this tax collector'" (Lk 18:11). He has so little self-confidence that the opinion of others takes more importance for him. "All their works are performed to be seen. They widen their phylacteries and lengthen their tassels. They love places of honor at banquets, seats of honor at synagogues" (Mt 23:5-7). The goal of the Pharisee is to *preserve* his image and live in such a way as to not commit any fault. What appears to be hypocritical reveals, in fact, that the Pharisee is incapable of accepting himself in his weakness. He needs to flaunt his virtues, his vows, his accomplishments. He needs to reiterate to himself the extent of being someone wonderful, extraordinary, and virtuous; furthermore, he seeks for others to follow him and admire him because, in the depth of himself, behind his shell, he feels fragile and very threatened.

Piet van Breemen gives an example that makes us understand the wound and the psychology of the Pharisee:

> Let us imagine a child who was never loved by his parents and sees other children showered with affection by theirs. He would be jealous and say: "I want to be loved also. I have never experienced it, but I will earn my parent's love, incite it by my good behavior." The child works at behaving in a perfect manner to *earn* the love of his parents. This is the Pharisee. He acts in such a way as to give birth to God's love. He, himself, takes the initiative. What a terrible world! What an impossible burden! Nonetheless, the whole perspective of the Gospel is about a child who has only ever experienced love and tries his best because he is loved. He commits errors at times, but they do not wound him terribly. They do not endanger the love given by his parents. The possibility of being unloved never enters his mind. For the Pharisee, the accent is placed on his own strength and his own deeds.[53]

[53] Piet van Breemen, *Comme le pain rompu* (Paris: Fayard, 1978).

Accepting to Confess

Accepting to confess is also a part of the long journey toward serenity. Is it not necessary to reconcile with one's past one day, to reconcile with oneself and to reconcile with God in order to die in peace? Confession is the response of a deep need in the human heart. Here I use the word *confession* or to *confess* and mean it in the wide sense of being truthful, to open up, to reveal one's life and one's past to someone else, without hiding anything, to take off one's mask. As a Catholic priest, I can only emphasize the sense of confessing to a priest and the role of confession, which has tended to be more and more without the means of individual confession. There is not always the sense of deep liberation that true confession brings by *verbalizing* before a human being our weaknesses and our sins, even the most secret ones and the most difficult to confess.

Heart Disease

Modern man suffers from heart disease: it is his conscience gnawing at him. I remember a man who came, sometime ago, to meet a priest, saying: "My doctor, who has been treating me for a year, said to me at our last visit: "You are Catholic?" "Yes." "Do you have faith?" "I think so," "Then I want to be honest with you...I can still prescribe tranquilizers to calm your anxiety but, in thinking about what you have said regarding your past, I need to tell you: Go and see a good priest, open up and confess yourself honestly to him, hiding nothing. In your case, it is possible that your anxiety will disappear."

After confession, this man was able to sleep and his anxiety disappeared. By relating this event, I do not want to imply that confession solves all problems and that the problems of anxiety are moral problems. However, I dare say that *some* persons have wounds in their conscience and, for those who have faith, *confessing* can be a significant factor for a true liberation.

Are We Immaculate?

One day, Bishop Fulton Sheen, the great American speaker and preacher, addressed an audience of official national and international Christians. Among them were bishops, superiors general, directors of movements, etc. He greeted these *elite* with these words, "Hello, dear sinners, colleagues!" It was amusing to see these Christians, these eminent pastors and these theology professors finding themselves ill at ease, with an uncomfortable laugh. And Fulton Sheen continued: "We don't like to hear about sin very much. Since some do not believe in the Immaculate Conception of the Virgin Mary anymore... we now believe in our own immaculate conception. There are no more sins for some of us... we only make mistakes." This is a true preacher who does not seek to be loved by his audience, nor seek to dazzle by the latest theological research, but wants to *convert* them. Everyone knows that Fulton Sheen succeeded in converting hundreds of persons, including radio and television celebrities.

As C. S. Lewis rightly said: "When man comes closer to God, he sees in a clearer way the evil that resides in him. When man debases himself, he has less and less consciousness of his pathetic situation. A man who is moderately evil knows that he is not really good; a man completely depraved thinks that he is perfect." We resemble the French man from Camus in *La Chute*. He mocks himself: "Monsieur, you see, my case is exceptional. I am innocent." But are we so innocent?

How difficult it is to genuinely recognize ourselves! We think that we are very good persons. When Saddam Hussein said: "I am a God-fearing man," one must think that he was undoubtedly convinced. Jean Claude Duvalier, the former dictator of Haiti said of himself: "I know that my people love me." We saw on television the arrest of the dictator of Romania and his wife Elena Ceausescu. To those who condemned her to death, she calmly affirmed: "You have no right...I am the mother of all." She was definitely self-assured!

Father Bernard Bro, a Dominican, related the shock he received from his novice master in 1945. It was the end of the war. In Europe, horrifying crimes of the Nazis were discovered, and one novice decried how terrifying it was that such individuals existed. Then the old master of novices looked at them attentively and after a long silence said to them: "My brothers, if you still do not know that you can do the same as these torturers, then you have understood nothing about humility." And Father Bro concluded: "Yes, in the depth of each one of us, we can become a monster."

In his book *The Nazi Doctors,* Robert J. Lifton gives some surprising examples of feigned innocence. He emphasizes that the atrocities of the Nazis were not committed by the most depraved, without education, but by honorable medical practitioners, by men of law, by members of the professional elite. Lifton recounts: "When I was questioning them, they generally presented themselves as reasonable people. They wanted me to confirm their self-image. They were unable to bear facing their culpability; therefore, they denied it, pretended to be innocent and cast the culpability outside themselves by accusing the system, 'the complex conditions in Auschwitz.'"[54]

This *simulated innocence* led them to a surprising blindness. Lifton wrote: "None of them, not one ex-doctor whom I addressed, came to a clear and moral evaluation of what they had done and their participation in that egregious system. They all denied their culpability."

It is strange how we all believe ourselves *innocent* and do not perceive our blindness. Accepting ourselves as sinners is not easy. We prefer to recognize ourselves as sinners *in general* and to receive a *general* absolution once or twice a year as opposed to being obliged to recognize ourselves as real sinners and admit to someone *what it consists of.*

[54] Robert Jay Lifton, *The Nazi doctors: medical killing and the psychology of genocide* (London: Macmillan, 1986).

Something Missing in the Interior

A philosopher related the story of a man who tried to hold a dead man erect. After several attempts, he gave up the task saying: "There is something missing inside." It is the story of everyone. A psychologist, a doctor, or a master can ease certain complexes, but no one can abolish the fundamental cause of all conflicts. Only God can do it by bringing to man what he cannot accomplish himself. If one has a moral illness that is sin, he will regain health only through the means instituted by God to give man back his spiritual peace.

Feeling guilty, many persons seek forgiveness by unconsciously spending their lives trying to *expiate*. Paul Tournier, a psychotherapist, explains this in the following:

> Some psychoanalysts have revealed that several illnesses, physical and emotional, and even some accidents or frustrations in social or professional life were, at times, attempts - entirely unconscious - at expiation of their culpability. It is a form of punishment that is self-administered by the victim and that repeats itself endlessly with a sort of pitiless fatality. They try in vain and unconsciously to expiate, to *pay*. They literally pay by their health.[55]

The conscious spirit cannot withstand the memory of shameful actions. It throws them into the subconscious, which then brings consequences to the body through anxiety. Jean Vanier explains how guilt sometimes becomes like a cancer that consumes a person from the inside:

> There are problems that originate in guilt or in an increasing uneasiness of the heart or conscience in a person. They cannot withstand having hidden an abortion or a sexual

[55] Paul Tournier, *Bible et médecine* (Delachaux et Niestlé, 1976); Paul Tournier, *A Doctor's Casebook in the Light of the Bible* (New York: Harper, 1976).

> relationship outside of marriage, or to have lied or been entangled in corruption. The guilt becomes like a cancer that consumes the interior of the person, paralyzing the joy and the light, preventing communion and sometimes cooperation until there is an explosion when the uneasiness becomes too great; it becomes a cry to find transparency, the truth about oneself.[56]

True and False Guilt

Jansenism and the puritanism of the past have perhaps contributed to eliciting guilt in persons who were not truly culpable but, consequently, today we believe ourselves innocent, without stain. A Christian psychologist, Carol Oden, in his article "Side Door to the Kingdom," does not fear to say:

> When a person tells you that they feel guilty, it is often because they are guilty. Perhaps they lived a tragic childhood, or were treated unjustly, or were led by circumstances into a situation where their heart was broken. For these, they are not culpable. But if they become sick emotionally afterward, it is because they are often guilty of reacting toward certain circumstances from the past in a way that it is not from God. If you observe a certain sick person carefully, you will notice that sometimes there is, underneath the illness, much resentment, with self-alienation and even hate. One needs to know that healing and health are often dependent on one's will to forgive the past, to accept oneself, to love truly and to be open to hope.

It is true that false guilt exists in our world. Psychoanalysis has shown this. Many people are tormented by false guilt. They are sometimes crushed by anxiety and shame or by a complex that does not imply a real fault.

[56] Vanier, *Toute personne histoire sacrée*; Vanier, *Our Journey Home*.

However, it is no less true that *pseudo-innocence* exists. It happens in those who believe themselves upright and just, when they do not believe their faults or transgressions are real, or they refuse to see them. In deep analysis, psychologists are more and more cognizant of this.

An American author, Dr. Sharon Hymer, a psychology professor in New York, published a volume, *Consuming Confession*,[57] of nearly three hundred pages on the *fundamental* need for a human being to *confess*, to *open up* to another person, *without hiding anything*. For many years, she investigated several hundred persons on the liberation brought about through *confessing* – without hiding their faults, their sins, and their innermost secrets. In fact, these persons had kept everything inside and it prevented them from living and feeling free. The author also studied *Catholic confession* with its liberating role through *personal* confession. Dr. Hymer had formerly published a brilliant work on the opening of the soul and heart in psychotherapy. Her book, *Confession in Psychotherapy*, which was released in 1988, brought her interviews on the radio and television throughout the United States.[58]

It would be interesting to conduct a sociological study in French Canada and in Europe to establish the relevance between the decrease in individual confession by Catholics and the increase of the need to consult a therapist or psychologist to confide and open one's heart.

It is true that revealing our secrets, without hiding anything, and really confessing our faults, is not something easy for our ego. In a letter to Jacques Rivière, Paul Claudel wrote: "I have never felt such revulsion and agony as what I experienced the day of my first confession."[59]

Pastoral and psychotherapeutic experiences have proved that enormous interior resistance renders self-knowledge very difficult.

[57] Sharon Hymer, *Consuming confessions: the quest for self-discovery, intimacy, and redemption* (Center City, Minn.: Hazelden, 1996).
[58] Sharon Hymer, *Confession in Psychotherapy* (New York: Gardner Press, 1988).
[59] Paul Claudel; Jacques Rivière; Auguste Anglès; Pierre de Gaulmyn, *Correspondance Paul Claudel-Jacques Rivière: 1907-1924, édition complète* (Paris: Gallimard, 1984).

Any individual feels instinctive repugnance at opening up in depth and seeing, even for a brief moment, their true reality. It is certainly difficult and humiliating to confess our faults down to the roots. However, would that not be the true path toward serenity and peace of heart? Let us listen to [Saint] Pope John Paul II on this subject: "I cannot insist enough on the necessity of confessing our faults in person followed by individual absolution. The people of God are not a flock with uniformity: each member is unique before God." Confessing our faults is certainly full of anguish because it involves the death of the "idealized image" that we wish to preserve. We do not want to open up and confess who we really are. Paul Ricoeur said: "The more authentic the guilt, the more it is self-concealed."[60] Therefore, sinning is to be deceived and to delude oneself, it is blinding oneself. Concealing, *hiding*, covering up, and avoiding confession is a characteristic of sin. It is strange to realize how many men and women can become *counselors* and never confess themselves, sometimes for many years. In his work, *Actualité de la fonction prophétique*, Arnold Uleyn speaks this way:

> Knowledge of other men and self-knowledge are not identical. Often, we realize that a person who sometimes deeply penetrates the psychology of others does not arrive at a true self-analysis. The self is deformed and tarnished by illusions. This illusory self-image built according to our desires, does not conform to the reality seen by others and especially by God. "For everyone who exalts himself will be humbled" (Lk 13:14). Our criticism of others can be exact and penetrating but, nevertheless, dismiss the reality. We point the finger at the sins of others but make exception for ourselves by inserting our case in parenthesis because we entertain an erroneous and idealistic viewpoint regarding our own personality. Who does not know some persons who find no problem in seeing themselves as sinners in general,

[60] Paul Ricoeur, "Esprit," *French Literary magazine*, 1954, 308.

> but who strongly protest when a specific misdemeanor is attributed to them? [61]

In reality, it is fairly easy to declare ourselves sinners in *general*, globally – undoubtedly too easy. It is this discovery of an innate need in ourselves to confess, to reveal ourselves before someone else, that the therapist Sharon Hymer reveals in her volume on confession, *Consuming Confession.* She explains that often a person starts to be liberated when they admit something that was *never* expressed before. "I have never said this to anyone – they confess at a certain moment – it was too difficult; I was too ashamed." And Sharon Hymer explains that a change is always produced when the *confession* is really engendered from *truth* and *sincerity*:

> Confessing oneself is to retrieve our true identity in revealing our most secret intimacy to another human being. . . Deciding to make a true and complete confession means that we cannot remain the same person after confession. Afterward, the difficulty in confessing is transformed into peace and joy. Revealing oneself to someone is taking a risk, but this risk liberates our interior prisons.

Pus Extraction

From the beginning, men have known that opening up and pouring out one's heart produces a *cathartic* effect. The feeling of repressed guilt poisons a man or woman. Confessing often has a therapeutic effect. In an article on the "Anthropological Value of Confession," Cardinal Danneels said: "It is when we bring the fault to our lips to express it that we recognize it. Before confessing, one has been wearing the fault inside; now one can see it from the outside – what is evil inside ourselves inspires a certain repugnance, a desire for distance. Confessing

[61] Arnold Uleyn, *Actualité de la fonction prophétique: psychologie pastorale et culpabilité* (Paris: Desclée de Brouwer, 1966).

nudges toward humility and all the spiritual riches available through this virtue."

It is known that Jung, the psychoanalyst, often sent his Catholic clients to confess to their priest. Therefore, I would like to insist on one fact: the act of confessing, *admitting*, brings evident psychological benefits linked to mental health. Following the thought of Sidney Jourard [62] and his disciples, we observe that persons who accept to reveal themselves, to confess, to say the truth to someone else instead of keeping everything inside, contribute to their mental health and well-being. In this way, they engage in a process of liberation, of self-forgiveness leading to reconciliation with themselves, which is the basis for reconciliation with others. However, even as confessing is liberating, the penitent who confesses must have in his spirit the thought that confession is not therapy, even if confession can have a therapeutic effect.

Even the Most Secret...

It is certainly for good reason that [Saint] Pope John Paul II returns unceasingly to the importance of a *personal approach* to *individual confession* and *absolution*. Before mentioning that the proposals of the Pope could be considered outdated, perhaps we should ask if he is not a *prophet*, and if he does not see better than we do the *signs of the times* which reveal to us the need to *confess and verbalize* what is hidden and, foremost, our sins, *even the most secret ones*. As I have mentioned before, when lay persons, university personnel, psychology professors and therapists write theses and volumes on the benefits of *admitting* and *confessing*, and that they do not fear respectfully mentioning Catholic confession, one should perhaps question oneself more deeply before launching into general absolution without confession. This is something to reflect upon! When a door is opened, it is not easy to close it. And when we meet persons who, during a retreat, confess

[62] Sidney Marshall Jourard, *La transparence de soi* (Sainte-Foy: Éditions St. Yves, 1985).

individually after ten, twelve, or fifteen years of *only* having ever received general absolution without confessing, one needs to seriously question these absolutions.

During his visit to Canada, Pope John Paul II made this declaration, which is still very current, to the episcopal conference:

> The communal renewal *must not neglect the personal approach* of the penitent and the *personal absolution.* If our faithful were to lose the sense of sin and of *personal* forgiveness, if they were unable to find enough available priests for this *essential ministry*, there would be lacking a *principal dimension* in the authenticity of their Christian life. The last synod, where many of us participated, highlighted the absolute necessity of penance in the sense of sin, and the request for forgiveness in the Sacrament of Penance combined with the personal accusation of sin to a priest.[63]

In a *personal* approach, the confessor receives the confession of the penitent who takes the time to *verbalize* his faults.

To Verbalize

Jean Vanier explains the role of confession in human and divine psychology in Sacramental Confession:

> Jesus gave his priests a very particular power which is to make him present in Forgiveness, so that we could verbalize our infidelity, verbalize our sin. Liberation begins as soon as we confess, as soon as we verbalize. However, it is not about verbalizing to anyone, and in any way, but verbalizing and admitting to the one who has received the gift to forgive in the name of Jesus, and who has received from the Church this power and ministry.

[63] Jean-Paul II, *Discours à la conférence épiscopale* (Ottawa: Sept.20, 1984); *Address of Pope John Paul II to the Episcopal Conference of Canada* (Chapel of the Convent of the Sisters of Charity, 20 September 1984).

It is certainly difficult and humiliating to admit our faults down to the roots. However, it is the unique way that brings us liberation and peace of heart.

It is certain that the act of confessing by truly admitting our sins is often overwhelming. It is useless to deny it. But it is precisely this sorrow that has great value. This suffering, this sadness, in admitting that we are proud, impure, jealous, self-centered – this humiliation at confessing our misery before someone – leads us to regret our past.

Father Bro writes:

> One can act as if the problem of confessing does not exist anymore. But it does exist. And to evade it is a betrayal to the extent that the restoration of our dignity is linked to beatitude by recognizing our true culpability. Those who sideline confessing, under the pretext of a renewal of confession, are mistaken and they wrong us. What would confession be without heartbreak, without humiliation and admission? To admit is to break down. Whoever voluntarily withholds something that he knows to be serious has not broken down. That is it. If one holds something inside because it seems humiliating or too difficult to express, then one does not break down and does not truly experience beatitude and the joy of forgiveness.

The Gospel pardons those who recognize themselves culpable, but on the contrary, arouses the consciousness of culpability in those who flatter themselves of being just. In the Gospel episode of the adulterous woman, Jesus does not deny the culpability of the woman, but he does not condemn her. Beforehand, however, to the accusers of this woman, he says another word to awaken their suppressed culpability: "He who is without sin throw the first stone." In reality, to recognize honestly and without duplicity that we have sinned – to recognize, in spite of appearances, that we are jealous, envious, dominating, egoistic, impure, attached to goods and money, self-sufficient, etc. – is the condition necessary to be liberated and obtain the forgiveness of God.

"He who conceals his sins prospers not, but he who confesses and forsakes them obtains mercy" (Prov 28:13). Such is the reversal that the story of the adulterous woman brings to light in a striking manner, but that can be found in all of scripture. In psychological terms, we can formulate it this way: "God erases a conscious culpability and brings to consciousness a suppressed culpability."

To Be Known Personally

In the magazine *Pastorale-Quebec* of March 19, 1994, Louise Caron-Grégoire wrote:

> In our world of box-office, soundtrack and Internet communications, it seems important to re-validate the individual form of the Sacrament of Reconciliation that accentuates the personal love that God has for his child: "I called you by name, you are precious in my eyes, you are mine and I love you." As one baptized, I feel having a fundamental right to be known personally, and to admit the truth before "someone," would be a liberation by being given a word of healing. No therapy is usually prescribed without a personal meeting between the doctor and his patient. For me, collective absolution remains that of an emergency situation. It deprives the penitent of his right to be heard personally by the minister of the Church and to receive from him a personal and liberating word. In truth, confessing affirms that, before being collective, sin is an individual reality: it is born in the heart of man.

However, in order for individual confession and absolution to be truly *liberating*, one needs to be honest, transparent and sincere, which is not always the case.

Admitting Becomes Indispensable

We are very fearful of facing our real culpability. The pharisaic side that lives in us leads us to suppress our faults and perceive ourselves as just. One believes himself pure and just because he fears the anguish that would reveal his repressed culpability. He is afraid to admit his guilt, and the more fearful, the more he needs to appear strong and hide his fault.

Karen Horney writes on this subject:

> The more desperate a man feels beneath his fears and defense mechanisms, the more he needs to cling to the illusion of being right, to be absolutely perfect, and to reject instinctively all allusion indirect or implied that there is something evil in him and the need to undo it.

Suffering from a feeling of guilt (and it could be a real culpability), this person will always fear being blamed. They will do everything to never be accused. They will develop behavior that protects them from all criticism in order to avoid the anguish of feeling guilty. Then they will appear before others with such a perfect demeanor that they become unassailable. Unconsciously, this person says to themselves: "I do not want to be unmasked at any price – I will never admit. If I am unmasked, I will be seen as I am, I will not be loved anymore, I will be rejected."

And admitting, which would be so liberating, becomes *unthinkable* to consider – rather die than confess. God, nevertheless, waits for us in confession. He proposes that we be true, disarmed and crumbling. Our pride, however, leads us to neglect confession. We prefer lying to ourselves than to opening up.

Forgiving Is Not Excusing

To attain serenity, interior peace, and self-reconciliation, we must have the courage to *express* the truth about our past.

Peace cannot be obtained by saying that everything is fine, that we should not feel culpable, and that sin does not exist. If we desire to reach a tranquil old age and die peacefully, we must be open to God's forgiveness and sincerely admit our faults.

Here, we need to avoid confusion. To forgive (to absolve) is not the same as to excuse, to understand, to close the eyes, to pass over or to clear away – that would mean not accepting certain facts, ignoring the real culpability, not taking it into account, justifying it. One must not confuse the concept of forgiving someone with that of reassurance or of liberating that person from feelings of guilt, by trying to stifle remorse. In this way, one denies the responsibility of that person and declares them partially or totally innocent. A man of a certain age who had killed in his youth, or a middle-aged woman who had an abortion at sixteen, eighteen, or twenty, does not need to be pronounced innocent, or for the priest to close his eyes by trivializing these faults. These persons need to confess the seriousness of their act and, through the minister of the Sacrament, feel that God is Mercy and can forgive everything, even the worst things, if a person recognizes their fault without minimizing it, and truly confesses it. Tradition calls it *contrition*, *confession*, and *reparation*. These are acts lived with sincerity, bringing true peace of the heart and serenity. We would need new Curés of Ars and some Padre Pios in the twenty-first century. The latter received the charism of reading souls, so that the *confession* of the penitent might be facilitated. The crowds, who waited several days before confessing to them, proved that human nature does not change, that man needs to admit and confess himself, and that accepting confession is the only road leading to joy and serenity.

One Does Not Judge

In order to consent to recognizing ourselves as sinners, we need to descend from our pedestal. We need to live an experience that leads us to poverty of heart. The most important experience is to accept ourselves with our wounds. We cannot help a poor one if we have not discovered our own poverty, and we cannot heal someone else's wounds if we have not been affected by our own particular wounds. Jean Vanier said:

> The prodigal son identifies himself with pigs. This is why he does not judge anyone. To him, everything is mercy, everything is grace. The elder son judges because he is not touched by his own wounds. He builds fences around himself and refuses to look at his misery. One can grasp God's mercy only when deeply affected by one's own misery. And when we have experienced this misery, we can judge no one, whoever he is.
>
> In the religious world, one can quickly have an identity fabricated by the view of others. The Pharisees had this identity. They were admired and feared, but within them there was emptiness. When Jesus showed them this emptiness, it unnerved their psyche and they did not accept it. Instead of questioning themselves, they wanted to get rid of this man who became too dangerous as he confronted them with their anguish and their nothingness. They were simply poor men, sinners like others, as poor as Mary Magdalene and Barabbas, but they hid themselves beneath their persona. They had built a world of appearances around themselves, a world of power and glory, and they did not accept being loved in their littleness and fragility.[64]

The Pharisee wants to justify himself through his works. And he joins with the unconsciousness in us that would like to *earn* and *merit* love. In our Western society, we are conditioned to look for justification by our works: one always needs *to prove their value.* Society tells us that to be accepted, one must succeed. Therefore, we exhaust ourselves striving to excel in order *to be admired.* There can be some

[64] Jean Vanier, *Conférence "L'accompagnement spirituel"* 1983.

compassion in us when we observe the Pharisee, and the proud one, with eyes of the heart that see further than appearances.

Brother Ephraïm wrote:

> I was severe with the proud ones for a long time until I became conscious that pride has its roots in the feeling of insufficiency: deprived of part of my power, I unconsciously invent it; I summon it from my imagination. Described here is the paranoid who sleeps in every man. When this personality trait takes a pathological turn, this deluded person believes themself to be of great *character* and not someone modest and humble. Generally, this type of person was crushed by their father in childhood. The father and educators robbed a potentially brilliant personality. The wound of childhood was added to the wound of original sin.[65]

What would have happened to Francis of Assisi, Ignatius of Loyola, and many others without the conversion that released them from egoism and narcissism? Let us not forget that the saints were all wounded creatures like ourselves. They had faults like ours and sometimes even greater faults. The more they advanced on their journey, the more they recognized themselves weak and sinners, and the more they desired their fragility to be known. It is the "I rejoice to be imperfect" of Thérèse of the Child Jesus.

Accepting to Be Like the Rest of Humankind

How to heal from our pharisaism? First of all, the Pharisee is often an individual who does not *really live*. He is dead in his heart, soul, and emotions. One needs to know that it is possible to go through life without realizing that one has been dead for a long time: one functions, rushes, and organizes. One manages their time, their relations, follows

[65] Brother Ephraïm, *Sept paroles pour un bonheur* (Nouan-le-Fuzelier, France: Éditions des Béatitudes, 1997).

the rules but, deep inside, something is dead, a piece of self, the part of the repressed child beneath a persona.

The true saints, purified from their ego, become the most human of humans, defenseless like children. They know how to laugh and cry, they have no one to please; then they are very free. A true saint is never pharisaical and, at the same time, he often disturbs us because we do not like men and women who are free. We sometimes find that they lack diplomacy or nuances. They speak the truth, sometimes like children, and as one knows, the truth is shocking.

We can be healed of our pharisaism by a bitter failure, an unexpected trial, a public humiliation, or even a *serious fault* that causes us to fall from the pedestal of our false virtue and our spiritual pride. In his *Seeds of Contemplation*, Thomas Merton has a great passage on pharisaism and spiritual pride:

> I ponder this disease of spiritual pride. This worm insinuates itself in the souls of all religious. Who among us is capable of doing good without finding some sweetness that distinguishes us from the common sinners? This disease is especially dangerous when it resembles humility. When a proud one believes himself humble, his case is desperate. This is a man who accomplishes many things. He has worked hard and arrived at a remarkable position of strength and abnegation. The pleasure that he feels in accomplishing difficult tasks leads him to think secretly: "I am a saint." This man burns with self-contentment and imagines it to be Divine love. He believes his pride to be the Holy Spirit. When he enters this path, the evil that self-contentment can commit in the name of God is limitless. He is so full of himself that he cannot bear the advice of others or the orders of a superior. When his desires are opposed, he says to himself: "I am persecuted by men who are unable to understand those led by God's spirit," and believing to

> be a martyr, he is ten times more obstinate than before. When this type of human thinks of himself as a prophet or a reformer, the consequences are very serious...He is able to harm religion and bring hate upon the name of the Lord.[66]

It is by accepting to be a sinner, accepting to have in oneself the capacity to do every evil, and to recognize this, that we slowly begin to be healed of our unconscious pharisaism. As Jean Vanier said, "We must accept the wolf within us, and release it from the cave where we have enclosed it." Recovering the child in ourselves and in our wounded heart leads us toward interior poverty and liberates us.

[66] Thomas Merton, *Semences de contemplation* (Paris: Du Seuil, 1954); Thomas Merton, *Seeds of Contemplation* (New York: New Directions, 1949).

The Prodigal Child

When deep in the mud I cry out my misery to you
You are rising up already you arise O My Father
And looking out for my step you await my return
Already you can not bear to be hurt by love

When all my sins agitate my heart
You already offer me the water of happiness
And you want to wash me you await my return
You are already sobbing your heart swelling with love

And when I return no matter which way
You run toward me already with both arms extended
And you give me the kiss of forgiveness once more
And you cry with joy and you dance O My Father

CHAPTER SIX

ACCEPTING TO BE MOVED

If I had to choose
between a wounded heart that suffers
but is open to tenderness,
and a heart that does not suffer
but is closed,
I would most probably choose to suffer.

William Faulkner

It is strange to realize that, in general, until puberty boys and girls both easily express their emotions and let their tears flow freely. Afterward, with boys, the tears suddenly stop, and it is a known fact that almost eighty percent of men between fifteen and fifty-five years of age have great difficulty in expressing their emotions by weeping, and in revealing their heart. For some men the beginning of old age is a flood gate, a sort of hollowed-out shell, and tears start to flow more freely again.

Do we need to attain old age to be moved? At what age have we closed our heart, repressed our emotions? What has happened long ago that we have become so cerebral, so rational, at least apparently? Jean Bastaire wrote: "Our heart of a child was tender. The trials poorly accepted have hardened it."

We rationalize, we harden ourselves, we freeze our emotions to repress a past suffering. When the needs of our child's heart have not been satisfied, we can sometimes find ourselves at fifty years old with the same needs – as strong as ever – as at seven years old. For example, a father who treats his child without affection, in a distant and cold manner, can create within him later the need to seek cold, cerebral, and rational people. As an adult, this child will have a fear of feelings. He will keep his distance. Through the fear of emotions, he may arrive at confusing the expression of feelings with sexuality. He will need to protect himself because he will fear his own body.

Once, a young man in his late twenties met with a counselor. His father had never expressed any feelings toward him. The young man said to the counselor – who wanted to help him in his life as a couple: "My lack of feelings does not disturb me. I live fine this way." The counselor answered him: "The dead have no feelings, and nothing disturbs them. In your case, you have killed all your feelings." He thought that his remark would shake the young man but, instead, he answered coldly, without emotion: "I know that I am dead. When I was younger, I would have liked to be cuddled because I had a terrible fear of death, a horrible fear. But no one came. I decided then, that if I were dead, there would be nothing to fear any longer. This is why I started considering myself as dead. I did not think that I would live until my twenties. I am very surprised to be still alive."

Do we not carry inside some wounds from the past, and sometimes from a long-ago childhood? In his inner depth, man needs to search beyond the appearances to ask himself these essential questions: "*Am I loved? Am I loveable?*" If a man refuses to return to the origin of his wounds, he risks remaining a prisoner of his affliction and of using a series of stratagems to defend his anxieties. Some persons are so afraid to touch their wounds that they say: "Why stir up all of this?" However, it is not by denying sufferings and by repressing one's own heart that one heals but, rather, by *entering* into *the inner self* and casting light, that one can become free. Many people conceal their heart, create a shell and wear masks to avoid entering into their heart and confronting their inadequacies and hidden sufferings.

Who has not hardened their heart and feelings? Who has not laid concrete over their wounds? Who has not repressed their heart of a child? "We are all more or less defectors from our childhood," wrote Jean Bastaire, "and we can try to forget the child that we have been, but the child does not forget and keeps vigil."

The Fear of Being Vulnerable

We are aware of the need to open our heart but, at the same time, we are afraid of what could happen. As Jean Vanier said very well: "We do not like being vulnerable, we are afraid of our fragility and we become hyperactive or depressed. We fill up each instant of our day because we cannot tolerate our vulnerability." We repress our woundedness, our feelings, and we freeze the tears that are hardened in us.

Dr. Artur Janov wrote:

> Tears wash sufferings and unmask the unconscious. One can say that tears are the prerogative of humankind. It is our aptitude for weeping and shedding tears that distinguishes us from animals. Weeping is a process of healing. However, in our society – for inexplicable reasons – weeping has been categorized. One tells children to stop crying, one treats them as whiners, one considers it to be more adult not to cry, and one regards tears to be a sign of weakness. Then one blocks this innate biological function. It happens that the suppression of tears has been instilled for such a long time that one cannot recover their tears. These cases are candidates for serious illnesses. I have observed

several allergies and illnesses disappear when my patients recovered their faculty of weeping.[67]

When facing an affliction or the memory of an old wound, the reaction of many is to protect themselves, to harden, and to repress this suffering in their inner depth. It is the fear of hurting, of suffering, as before.

Confronting Our Own Wound

If we have not met our heart of a wounded child, we can help no one because it is the *false-self* that the other will meet. To become empathizing, one needs the ability *to be touched* by the person whom we are meeting. In the Gospel, Jesus allowed himself to be touched; he is "seized with pity" and is "moved with compassion." He presents himself as a sensitive man, with deep feelings that he is unafraid to express.

"When Jesus saw that she was weeping and the Jews who had come with her weeping, he became perturbed and deeply troubled and said, 'Where have you laid him?' They said to him, 'Sir, come and see.' And Jesus wept. So the Jews said, 'See how he loved him'" (Jn 11:33-36).

"Jesus wept." At this moment of profound emotion, Jesus lets his tears flow. He weeps. He weeps because he is moved. He weeps because Mary wept, and he is touched by her tears. Jesus does not protect himself. He gives us an example of a man, very masculine, strong, perfectly human and sensitive who does not, however, suppress his heart and emotions, but shows them publicly. He weeps because tears belong to the humanity he assumed. "Real tears," writes the theologian Olivier Clement, "reveal that, in dire situations, there are no great persons." When one weeps, one exhibits the heart of a child, and Jesus demonstrates it, he, who told us to become "small like

[67] Artur Janov, *Le nouveau cri primal: revivre et vaincre sa souffrance* (Paris: Presses de la Renaissance, 1992). Artur Janov, *The New Primal Scream: primal therapy twenty years later* (London: Abacus, 1993).

a child." All the psychologists say that the ability to face our feelings, and freely express our emotions, is an indication of affective maturity and mental equilibrium. One who is unable to express their emotions is often a prisoner of an old wound that, through fear, prevents them from being themselves. They take refuge in their head in order to protect their heart.

To help others, we need to be in touch with our own heart. We cannot genuinely help another without penetrating his heart and it is with our own heart that we achieve it. In the Gospel, Jesus empathizes because he is a perfectly integrated man, including the sensitivity and emotions of man. According to an anonymous English author mentioned by Adler, to genuinely help another, one needs to "see with the eyes of the other, listen with the ears of the other, and feel with the heart of the other." This means to understand them not only intellectually, but emotionally, with one's own being, a meeting of heart-to-heart, with an intuitive ability to imagine the suffering of the other, even if they cannot express it outwardly. Let us speak of *empathy*. In its current use, this word means affection and warmth, like sympathy, but, in addition, the understanding of the *emotional* state of others. It is surprising to realize that the persons most apt to help others are those who are close to their own heart, who have suffered, who have their own wounds, and do not deny their humanity. These persons arrive at an *intuition* of the heart that diplomas and studies sometimes cannot achieve.

Many individuals have even written theses about helping and relationships with people, but it often remains theoretical. Persons feel it, but do not open up. One does not open their heart to a computer even if the computer is the best of computers. By thinking only logically and intellectually, one is unable to reach persons in the depths of their heart and hidden emotions.

In *A l'écoute de la désespérance*, Dominique Casera gives some characteristics of one who becomes a helper, whether he is a professional or not:

> He owes his ability with others to his interior security. Being very assured, he accepts himself with his wounds. He knows himself intimately and has a positive and loving attitude toward himself. He does not fear being touched by his emotions. He has confidence in himself and relies on his reactions. He perceives himself in a positive and joyous way without defending himself against spontaneity. He is not anxious about maintaining rigid control in the unfolding of a meeting or trying to avoid surprises in a developing relationship with another. He is simple, spontaneous, not defensive, and does not have a professional image to defend, nor a persona to preserve. He trusts his own impulses, accepts the spontaneous responses that surface within him and enjoys his interior security. He manifests openness in absorbing others' experiences.[68]

In order to truly help, one needs to be close to one's heart, accept one's humanity, and accept having a heart. Can one who has never wept understand fully the cries of another? To be compassionate is accepting to be deeply touched, if needed, moved to tears. One must not fear emotions and one needs to *suffer with* the other. Compassion cannot be taught: a child can become compassionate, and a great intellectual can harden his heart. One can even be charitable, so to speak, without being *seized with compassion.* Compassion is something that emanates; it cannot be taught. It is not the fruit of technique or study. The Gospel always uses it passively: *one is seized with compassion,* wanting it or not, deeply moved by the suffering of another. Our eyes become moist with tears and the other, in perceiving it, is also moved in turn. Then, there is a meeting of heart-to-heart, wound-to-wound. The mask has fallen, and the child of long ago appears in its fragility.

If we desire an example of *compassion* in the Gospel, we can read again the episode of the father and his two sons in Luke, chapter five.

[68] Dominique Casera, *Les psychotiques: à l'écoute de la désespérance* (Montréal: Éditions Paulines, 1978).

"While he was still a long way off, his father caught sight of him and was filled with compassion. He ran to his son, embraced him and kissed him." Let us notice that it is the father who *runs* to his son. He catches sight of him while the son is *still a long way off.* He runs. He lets himself be moved. The father urgently needs to show his son how he, the father, is in need of him. He becomes vulnerable like a child. He accepts his heart. His behavior, full of emotions, is surprising. A prominent man of the Middle East in those days, a man who respects himself, would never run anywhere in a flowing robe. Running is to lose one's dignity, in a certain sense, making a fool of oneself.

Let us observe these sensitive gestures, full of affection, of this father toward his son. How old was this son, seventeen, nineteen, twenty-three or more?

The Father and the Son's Identity

In a certain way, this father of the parable expresses almost *maternal* gestures. As mentioned by psychologists, this man assumes his *anima,* his feminine side, all his affection, and, in this sense, he is a true man who does not need to be *macho* to prove his masculinity. In his acclaimed painting, *The Return of the Prodigal Son,* Rembrandt expresses it admirably. He gives the father a masculine hand and a feminine one.

The father of the parable conveys an extraordinary tenderness which seems surprising in a man. He allows his shell and the attitude of a strong, powerful and masculine man to fall off. He *is moved.* He runs, gasping, emotional like a teenager, or an impetuous child; he opens his arms, he tenderly embraces his son to his heart, to his fatherly breast, and he kisses him, "covers him with kisses," as it is sometimes translated. He makes himself small, he leans down to his son, to his level in a way. This father exposes his heart. He lets his emotions speak for themselves without a word, without verbalizing, because he is so emotional. The father becomes almost more vulnerable than the son. He accepts his sensitive heart. One can almost say that, with the return of his son, the father reclaims the spontaneity of the heart of a child that he has perhaps not demonstrated for a long time. Do all these gestures of tenderness (running toward his son, embracing him and kissing him, etc.) not resemble the language of a child who, before speaking, expresses emotions through gestures?

How overwhelmed is the heart of the father! How many men and boys have never been embraced by their father? The father in this gospel of Luke lets himself be interiorly moved by the return of his son. "My heart is overwhelmed; my pity is stirred" (Hos 11:8). This son may have never met his father in an *affective* manner, may have never, or almost never, been *moved* by his father – father *lacking*, son *lacking*. Guy Corneau mentioned correctly, therefore, that the father of the parable let his emotions speak without trepidation. One can say that the father, in affirming his son, gives him back his life, bringing him into the world again by restoring him to the fullness of a son's life. The son needs to *feel* with all his being, and even in his manly body, the love and forgiveness of his father. Then, after the shell has fallen, the father enters into a heart-to-heart relationship with the son of his bosom.

It is sad to realize that sometimes good fathers, very loving, with a warm nature, often have apprehension in expressing their affectivity and tenderness toward their sons for fear that they could someday become effeminate or homosexual. However, the *contrary* is true because some homosexual sons, in their confidential admissions, often complain that their father was cold and distant with them, and that their mother was almost too good and invasive toward the son and smothered him to the point that no woman could be *his* woman. This son will often seek in a man the missing masculine affection. One must certainly not generalize, and many factors enter into account in searching for the identity and the "broken image"[69] produced in childhood, but I mention here this discovery of psychoanalysis

[69] Find more on this topic: Leanne Payne, *L'Image brisée* (Le Mont Pèlerin, Suisse: Éditions Raphael, 1996).

about the role of the father concerning the *identity* that a child, son or daughter, will adopt for themselves.

Returning to the parable of the father and his prodigal son with their moving and warm encounter, I would say, that at the heart-to-heart moment of the son and the father, there is nothing cold, distant and cerebral anymore in the attitude of the father. We can observe that this father, full of tenderness, is very different from so many fathers who are closed off from their sons or daughters. This father who runs, weeps, and embraces his son is profoundly touched. He acts spontaneously, without too much reflection, without calculating, because something happened that moved him to compassion. This father lets himself be touched: *touched* with compassion. In other words, compassion allows him to leap, all at once, over the distance that the son created between them, and his gestures (running, embracing, kissing tenderly) are the concrete removal, created by compassion, of this distance.

Accepting to have a heart opens us to compassion. "Compassion," as Lytta Basset writes, "consists in hearing in the other the child who weeps, even if he cannot hear it himself."[70] In order to hear *the child who weeps in the other*, our heart must accept to be wounded and not seek refuge within a shell.

Today, there are so many persons, so many young people, who do not love themselves and do not *feel* loved. What has been missing? Doctor Anna Terruwe, psychotherapist and committed Christian, expresses it this way in her book *Amour et équilibre:*

> Love must be detectable in facial expressions, in posture, in movements. The typical characteristic of the psychic motor function of love is the tenderness proper to each expression of love. It can be manifested through looks, the sound of a voice, the words pronounced, the way of caressing. It is difficult to define tenderness with words, but one can describe it. Whoever is tender sees the other as someone

[70] Lytta Basset, *La joie imprenable* (Genève: Labor et Fides, 1996).

> good, beautiful and precious. The one who is tender is, in his heart, completely absorbed by the other and is happy with him. Tenderness is love even on the physical, corporal side. Whoever is tender is loving and whoever is loving is tender.[71]

The father of the prodigal son demonstrates his tenderness through all his *corporal* being. We know that love needs to be expressed through looks, touch and words. It is through the eyes that we first express esteem for someone, and that we love them. One can read the soul in the eyes; the eyes betray the intimate feelings of someone: the expression is soft, tender, joyful, sad, anxious, energetic, enthusiastic, reserved. In the eyes, without erring, one can perceive the inner disposition of a person, one can detect the influence of feelings. And love expresses itself in the same manner.

"You are somebody for me...You are precious in my eyes, and I love you," we read in the Bible. When we accept our heart, our sight is illuminated and allows the perception of love and sincere tenderness.

Sight is essential in human communication. It is first in the look of another that we discover ourselves as lovable. The other (father, mother, a true friend, spouse, grandfather, grandmother), in looking at us with love, allows us a discovery that moves us deeply and gives us new life; at that moment, we are the most important person for him or her. We discover ourselves in the gaze of the other.

Xavier Le Pichon explains:

> Every one of us, I believe, has had the experience of someone who gazed at us with love. We have perhaps said: "There is something in me that I have not discovered and that is in my depth, that attracts this love." It is an extraordinary mystery: in our inmost essence, the deepest part of ourselves, we need someone who reveals a communication

[71] Anna Albertina Antoinette Terruwe, *Amour et équilibre* (Paris: Apostolat des éditions, 1969).

> of love. We need another revealing to us that we are created for love, and by welcoming us, it is sensed in this way. The senses allow us to communicate. Love is communicated through the senses. One must understand this well and understand it in prayer. It is true even with the mystics. One communicates with the body and all the senses.[72]

When the Heart Becomes Tender

Our world, cold and rational, is thirsty for human warmth and tenderness. *Tenderness* stems from the adjective tender, which expresses the phenomenon that happens when a cold or hard heart of a man or woman becomes sensitive and vulnerable, when a *heart of stone* becomes a *natural heart* (Ez 36:26). Flesh and tenderness have this in common: vulnerability. Accepting to have a heart is to let oneself be moved from the inside. In tenderness, it is our heart of a child that meets the other's heart; in tenderness, two weaknesses resonate and recognize each other.

Tenderness enters through the body, the look, the touch and the attitude. In our erotic and hypersexualized world, one can sometimes confuse tenderness with a gesture of sexual connotation. Hélène Brunschurg, a psychologist says:

> We are acquainted with fathers and mothers who do not dare to express their attachment to their youngsters by tender gestures. Tenderness presupposes being at ease with one's sexuality. It joyfully accepts closeness with the body without a second thought. Some people do not express tenderness because they fear crossing, unconsciously, from a tender caress to a shameful sexuality. They mistakenly confuse erotic and sensual pleasure with affectionate tenderness. Tenderness, however, is fundamental in human

[72] Xavier Le Pichon, *Communication et communion* (Trosly-Breuil: Éd. de l'Arche, 1988). [https://vies-consacrees.be/xavier-le-pichon.html]

> relationships, between friends, parents and children, brothers and sisters, etc. Tenderness is not different depending on the sexes. You can be tender with whomever you want, man or woman, father or mother, son or daughter. It is perhaps, between grandparents and grandchildren that tenderness is easiest and least threatening. Our world needs tenderness.

In another text, this psychologist relates how much the tenderness of her grandfather influenced her in childhood and as a young person:

> What memories the word tenderness evokes in my heart. In our family, many persons were at times spirited and quick-tempered, nevertheless, it is their tenderness that I remember. My grandfather had treasures of tenderness for each one of us. He read us stories, cuddled us, and recounted memories of old times, notably of his mother (whom I have also met and whose tenderness melted us). He looked at us with so much love that sometimes a tear clouded his eyes. At times, he took my hand and held my face close to his with such fervor that I knew I was in his heart forever, as he was in mine. This undeniable tenderness extended throughout my life, to myself, my husband and my children.[73]

What happiness for a young boy or girl to have known such a chaste and affectionate tenderness in childhood and teenage years! One's whole life is influenced by it, giving an emotional equilibrium that is so rare these days.

Jesus, Tenderness and the Body

As Christians, we have believed too often that emotions are dangerous and that tenderness is suspicious. However it is not displayed this way

[73] Hélène Brunschurg, *Alliance*, number 91, February 1994.

in the Gospel. We have certainly read the Gospel, but too frequently in a cerebral manner.

How did Jesus use his body and his human fragility to communicate with people in the Gospel? The first striking observation, as we read it, is that Jesus communicates with *all his being.* One cannot say that it is a word, a look, a touch; it is the *whole person.* One of the most beautiful examples is given in chapter thirteen of the Gospel of John: *the washing of the feet.* Jesus enters into communication with his gestures, his body, his touch, his whole being. He desires to communicate his new commandment: "Love one another as I have loved you." Jesus sets aside his outer garments, ties a towel around his waist, and kneels down at their feet. He washes their feet, one by one.

In this event, we realize that Jesus is not a prisoner of his position. He does not affect a persona. Jesus kneels, he makes himself small and poor. The apostles see him, whom they call Master, taking off his garments, holding a towel and water. It is a communication through *sight.* Then he kneels at the feet of each, and the communication is now by *touch.* Jesus *touches* the feet of each, washes their feet with tenderness, and wipes them with the towel; it is a communication by *touch.* One can observe that the sight and touch come before the words. There is nothing abstract or cerebral in this episode. Everything is concrete; everything is conveyed through the body, in silence through gestures. It is first the look, then the touch, and the words only serve to make concrete the preceding gestures.

All in Tears

In the Gospel, Jesus teaches us another lesson on communicating with people. He allows others to reach him in *their* own way. For example, let us remember the event concerning a woman, a sinner of the city, in chapter seven of Luke's Gospel. This woman, full of emotion and sensitivity, this sinner, enters the banquet room. "Bringing an alabaster flask of ointment, she stood behind him at his feet weeping and began to bathe his feet with her tears. Then she wiped them with her hair, kissed them, and anointed them with the ointment." All these gestures from the heart, all these human gestures, sensitive and affectionate from this woman, Jesus allows with an extraordinary interior freedom. He allows her to kiss his feet and to weep. He does not intervene to stop her tears nor her affectionate gestures. One knows that the tradition and good manners of that time did not permit a woman to loosen her hair in public before a man. Untying the hair was perceived as a sensual gesture that scandalized several guests. Kissing the *naked* feet of Jesus, spreading perfume, and drying them with untied hair was not permissible. "He should know what sort of woman is touching him," said Simon. In spite of it all, Jesus is at ease, lets himself be touched and perceives the beautiful heart of this woman. He sees beyond the gestures, and therefore allows this affectionate woman (the sinner of the city) to communicate with him through her body, in *her* own way: perfume, kisses, loosened hair, touching – and all of this with tenderness and respect. Jesus lets her do it because what is important for him is what she conveys through these gestures. This event is filled with emotions and tenderness. Being human is to be moved by emotion, it is accepting to have a heart.

"Looked at Him and Loved Him"

We also know this episode of the rich young man. At a certain point, one can read: "Jesus looked at him and loved him." From the first moment of their encounter, the *look* of Jesus penetrates the depths of the heart of this young man and perceives his basic goodness, his beauty. He then calls this young person to become who he truly is because he is hiding under his possessions, his persona. Jesus *looked at him and loved him.* In fact, one says to someone "I love you" through the eyes before saying it with words. There is first a communication through the eyes before the words. The words communicated by the lips are what the heart sensed through the look. One loves through the eyes before loving through words. A child *feels* loved with the eyes before a word is said. Jesus looks at this youth and, with his look, wants his affection to be perceived. Abbe Caffarel once said: "What brings a human being to love himself is, first of all, that he is loved by another, and it is in the look of the other that he discovers himself loveable."

Positive Look

A Christian psychologist, Catherine de Guillebon, who worked at the *L'Arche* of Jean Vanier for several years, wrote the following about this look:

> The positive look is that look which intentionally sees the beauty, potential and value of another. Filled with wonder, this look is chaste and genuine. This look does not deny the weaknesses and obscurities of the one he sees. Furthermore, this look affirms that no evil, no wounds, no difficulties, nor sins, whatever the extent, have the last word: each time it is chosen, love is stronger than evil and death. In it, the Christian recognizes a gift of God, the Creator of love. The heart of the one created is beautiful and good and is called to eternal life. This is why the look of the Christian must become the look of Christ.

Call to Tenderness

In the Bible, if Jesus reveals himself as a tender being, he invites us to offer this same tenderness toward the persons that we meet. "Tenderness," says Pierre Talec, "is the genius of love; between persons, in silence, it gives the tonality of love's dialogue."

Tenderness manifests itself only in a climate of sincerity and trust. A hypocrite cannot be a creature of tenderness because his heart is *false* (Hos 10:2), like his face. Genuine tenderness is part of the truth. Accepting to open one's heart is the beginning for becoming more and more a being of tenderness. It is through tenderness that one becomes a person of communion. How is it that, in front of some persons, one does not feel their heart? They say what they mean but their words do not reach us – it is only words. Anna Terruwe, the psychotherapist, expresses it this way:

> First, the look cannot lie. In the eyes one can read the soul; the eyes betray the intimate feelings of a person: the look is cheerful, sad, tender or energetic. In the eyes one can see without error the intimate disposition of a person because, in each expression of the eyes, one can discover the consequences of the felt emotion. One can feel genuine affection by the tonality of the voice and by the words that express something. Gentleness, tenderness and love express themselves in tonality: even an animal feels affection in the tonality of his master's voice. As for the look, the tonality of voice is determined by feelings and can hardly be influenced by the will. In arising solely from an act of the will, without adequate tonality, words, beautiful as they are, do not resonate as "true," really human, and do not feel sincere. The will and the feelings of the heart must be in harmony; a human being is both spiritual and provided with senses. He expresses himself spontaneously through words, which are both spiritual and sentient.[74]

Why are emotions so frightening to church people? The virtue of chastity should not be a repression of affection and sensitivity, nor a fear of the body and sexuality. As noted previously, the word of Pascal is true: "Whoever wants to act the angel acts the beast." Experience shows more and more that, often, human beings who *have repressed* their emotions, *frozen* their tenderness, disdained their body and their sexuality through a false ascesis or discarnate spirituality – after many years of apparent superhuman perfection – suddenly *crack under the*

[74] Anna Terruwe, *Amour et équilibre*.

surging of all the repressed affectivity. This affectivity explodes like a furious volcano.

Do we consider teaching courses on *affectivity* in our seminaries and novitiates of religious communities in order to not fear, but integrate, our affectivity – without repressing it – with calm and serenity? I wrote in an article that, in the future, we need priests of mercy with the heart of a child, and I dare say, bishops with the heart of a child, and religious who are comfortable in their skin, who having accepted their feminine side and characteristics as women, do not need to seek power for the sake of power, and claim a false masculine equality. Fortunately, such consecrated persons who are comfortable in their skin already exist, and more than we think, and it is wonderful.

The Heart of Paul

We can open the letters of Saint Paul to realize how much affectivity and feelings surge forth in these pages. "Rather, we were gentle among you, as a nursing mother cares for her children. With such affection for you, we were determined to share with you not only the Gospel of God, but our very selves as well, so dearly beloved had you become to us" (1 Thes 2:7-8). Paul does not fear to demonstrate his tenderness and his affectivity; he truly accepts having a heart. For him, the agape, love and charity, call for the richness of great sensitivity without being sentimental. "Yes," writes Paul to the Corinthians, "for out of much affection and anguish of heart I wrote to you with many tears, not that you might be pained but that you might know the abundant love I have for you" (2 Cor 2:4). "For I have already said that you are in our hearts, that we may die together and live together" (2 Cor 7:3). This spiritual paternity of Paul expresses itself by words so full of tenderness that we also feel today this human heart of the apostle: "It is right that I should think this way about all of you, because I hold you in my heart...how I long for all of you with the affection of Christ Jesus"

(Phil 1:7-8). And in Galatians 4: "My children for whom I am again in labor...I would like to be with you now." (Gal 4:19-20).

How beautiful it is to feel the human heart of Paul, filled with God's tenderness and unafraid to express himself warmly.

It should be a lesson for us in proclaiming ourselves Christians and disciples of Christ's love, even if it is possible that in our education – without much demonstration of human warmth and with a certain cerebral puritanism that fears the language of the heart – we might not have dared to express our affection and may have had a lack of simplicity and spontaneity in our human relationships.

We can even intimidate persons we meet because they may think that we are different from them and too distant, as if we were *above* their humanity, and that witnessing to the Gospel, instead of causing us to be more human and welcoming, seems to render us colder and more distant. As we know, many young people and even adults have suffered from a lack of human warmth in their family relationships, in particular from their fathers, and sometimes suffer for many years.

True love which has its roots in God, and carries itself in charity, expands the heart. Through a heart burning with God's love, a true saint becomes more and more *human* and often, in maturity and old age, more so than in his youth. In fact, with all his affectivity being integrated and purified in the Holy Spirit who is Love, he becomes unafraid of his heart and his body because he knows himself to be inhabited by the tenderness of another, the *Other.*

A God Who Is Stirred

The Bible is filled with feelings and emotions. The theme of compassion, for example, returns often: "As a mother comforts her son, so will I comfort you" (Is 66:13). In the Bible and even more in the New Testament, God has a heart, a human heart. Christ is God but is also human. He is one hundred percent human. In Jesus Christ, God has a human heart that is stirred with emotions. In our times, should we not renew devotion to the Sacred Heart of Jesus by demonstrating the humanity of God made flesh? God has a *human* heart united with his divinity. In the Gospel, Christ expresses his compassion toward men and women in distressing situations, along with poverty-stricken individuals, to the extent that he considers done to himself what we do for the least and most suffering of his brothers (cf. Mt 25:31-40).

Jesus is not afraid of his heart. He accepts it totally. In our Western culture, intellectual and rational communication seems respected and feelings appear to be suspect, especially in the religious world. "I think, therefore I am," said Descartes, meaning to put the heart aside. Modern psychology has rediscovered the aspect of the heart, the feelings, the unconscious, and the emotions, for human balance and maturity. Feelings and emotions are recognized and accepted by Christ even while highly intellectual individuals around us are mocking feelings. In our liturgies, under the pretext of purification and simplicity, addressing the body, the senses, and the emotions is often left out. Incense, lights, the colors of chasubles, beautiful music and meaningful gestures are disappearing to make room for simplicity that addresses minds more than the physicality and sensibility of creatures.

In the episode of the sinner in Luke 7, we see that Christ does not reject the emotions and feelings that scandalize the Pharisee. "If this man were a prophet, he would know who and what sort of woman this is who is touching him" (Lk 7:39). Notice the words "who is touching him" and a sort of *disdain for the body* and for *touch* by the intellectual Simon the Pharisee. Christ is not afraid of emotions; he admires the human feelings of this woman: he senses all goodness in her and the desire for a genuine and chaste relationship in the most beautiful sense of the word. He foresees her desire for a true and purified affective communion. Christ forbids himself all judgement. He is the most human of humans. He is God incarnate. Therefore, by feeling in himself all the gamut of feelings and emotions – positive and negative – present in the men and women that he meets, he recognizes their value. He accepts his human heart and by accepting himself totally, in experiencing himself as a man, in appreciating himself freely, he accepts, experiences, and appreciates others. Amidst men and women of his time, he fully accepts himself as a man, and thus understands the humanity of others. Totally open to himself and his heart and totally open to others, he then welcomes them without judgement or condemnation.

At the beginning of this book, I mentioned that we must accept to be human. To be human is also to accept having a heart because I do not think that we can be compassionate toward others if we are not in contact with our own heart, our emotions, our wounds and our poverty. We can only approach the fragility of another through our own fragility.

He Has Taken Our Infirmities

Our Western theology has often lost sight of the dimension of God's *compassion* toward our misery. The presence of God becomes personal and tangible through the human person of Christ. "And the Word became flesh and made his dwelling among us" (Jn 1:14). God made himself small and vulnerable and passed through the gamut of human experiences. As mentioned by a theologian:

> Christ truly identifies, without reserve, with the destiny of the unfortunate as if he were taking their place. One must conclude that this Man is so human that he, mysteriously but truly, made the place and destiny of each man his own... He refers to a substitution that largely includes what the Church will later call the Incarnation.[75]

To Be Affirmed by Another

Tennessee Williams, an American playwright, declared: "No one is valuable before being loved." We all have the need for another to reveal

[75] Théodore Preiss, *La Vie en Christ* (Paris: Delachaux et Niestle, 1951).

us to ourselves, to affirm and confirm us. "This is my beloved son, with whom I am well pleased," said the Father to his son Jesus prior to his desert experience at the beginning of his mission. We all have the need for someone to tell us: "You are my beloved son, my beloved daughter, you are somebody for me." Jean Vanier comments on this passage that sometimes resembles a second birth or a rebirth of the heart and the entire being:

> This passing or this conversion often has its origin in the meeting with a person who has recognized our inner beauty, who has grasped the secret of our being beneath our faults, our fears, our false values, and sees the life potential contained in this secret.
>
> For me, this meeting occurred with Father Thomas who welcomed me after all those years in the Marines. I had the impression that he knew, that he perceived, all the good or bad within me – my secret – and that he loved me as I was. It was liberating for me. It is wonderful to be seen, to be recognized as a unique person who has a destiny and a mission. It is wonderful to feel that someone has confidence in you, that you are not judged, condemned or devalued but loved; that one does not need to prove oneself. One can let the masks and the fences fall.

And Jean Vanier explains how much confidence is needed to really open up:

> It is healing to tell everything to this other whom we trust, who welcomes us fully with all the brokenness and wounds inside of us, with all the culpability of the past. The word is liberating. In front of this other who accepts us, the hidden child is liberated. Finally, one has the right to be himself with his past and does not need to hide anymore. For some persons, this human being who reveals us to ourselves

can be a friend, an aunt, a master, a priest, an educator, a psychologist or a spiritual guide.[76]

In our present society, who will be a reliable *source* of hope so that pure water often buried under the mud of our hearts is capable of flowing out? Who will be true spiritual guides, spiritual fathers and mothers who, without dominating or possessing the other, will affirm in individuals what is most beautiful in each one? The future of the world depends on this.

Witnesses Alive

In my ministry, I sometimes meet people from all ages, including young people. What surprises me with the young generation of today (thirty or less) is to realize that the teenage years sometimes seem to be prolonged up to twenty-five or thirty years old and, in view of affective and identity balance, to what extent these young people are fragile and wounded in their hearts. Often, they are unable to freely open up to another person. However, despite their astounding ignorance of the basics of Christian faith, they have hearts that are poor because of their sufferings and are open to Jesus Christ's salvation when it is presented by true witnesses of the Gospel.

I sincerely believe that these young ones need what I would call a pre-evangelization of the heart. There is a certain language, an attitude from some men of the Church and some Christians, that does not reach them anymore. I am convinced that this new generation of pagans can say "yes" to the Good News, as in the time of Saint Paul, but cannot discover the Good News of the Gospel if they are in contact solely with cold Christians, cerebral and distant Church men, or rigid and anxious women. Even with blue or orange hair and rings piercing their bodies, these young people also need to meet lively witnesses of the Gospel, men and women close to their heart. In his volume *L'Expérience Dépressive*, Dr. Yves Prigent, a psychiatrist, stated powerful words

[76] Vanier, *Toute personne histoire sacrée*; Vanier, *Our Journey Home.*

on certain attitudes of some Church men, words that should not be rejected but listened to:

> I noticed that clergy who spoke to me about religion were mostly learned, almost always dominating, and often virtuous. But it did not appear that they were fervent lovers, children ablaze, beautiful living creatures of the resurrection morning, beings carried by the great wind of desire unfurled at Pentecost. Their existence did not appear to me as adventurous, intensely free, profoundly animated, far-reaching, very open, passionately inventive, as conscious men might have been whose incarnate desire brought them to a death, therefore to more life through resurrection. On the contrary, it appeared to me that what was of the religious domain was withdrawn, rigid, pre-formatted, pre-digested, pre-considered, felt by someone else. There was no earnest doubt, no bursting folly, no disturbing momentum, no childlike logic, no natural beauty that showed me that the God of these persons was alive, full of desires, gracious, intoxicating like bread and wine, passionate like a good shepherd or fiancé.[77]

We need a return to spontaneity, to that enthusiasm of a young heart. "One can see well only with the heart," said the Little Prince of Saint-Exupery. We need to abandon our rigidity and our shells.

True Fathers and the Freedom of Saints

Our world needs true spiritual fathers, as opposed to gurus or domineering personalities, who use the immaturity of the young in order to manipulate them. Since our society has suffered from paternalism at times, it often rejects true paternity. However, how society is awaiting true fathers! Olivier Clément has this reflection:

[77] Prigent, *L'Expérience dépressive.*

> People are searching for real spiritual fathers able to welcome them, to love them, to make them understand that each person is worthy of love because most people are in need of love. Some have the impression that no one loves them and end up doubting and hating themselves.
>
> What people await from Churches are spiritual fathers. A spiritual father is one who, from his look and presence, warms you and lets you see that you are loved. Then, one first believes that they are loved by him and he lets it be known that through him, it is Someone else.

True saints are not awkward or rigid. We can think of Philip Neri, running and laughing in the streets of Rome with a group of youngsters, cutting his beard only on one side to make them laugh, and not taking himself too seriously. Think of Don Bosco making somersaults and performing acrobatics with the teenagers of Turin; Benedict Labre, the beggar of God, wandering the streets and sleeping under bridges; Francis of Assisi, the prince of poets, passing "for a fool in the world," as he said; and Father Henri Roy, founder of the Canadian J.O.C., visiting miserable prisons and starting projects without a penny in his pocket. This is the folly of saints who are not awkward or rigid but supremely free and open. They are men and women incarnate who, having accepted their heart, are witnesses of God's tenderness which our world has so much need of. Let us pray to the Holy Spirit to give us such true witnesses.

Do Not Complain Too Much

Do not complain too much about having a heart of flesh
Your eyes will be more beautiful when you cry
From your tears will be born a fruit of the earth
An unknown flower we have not breathed in

Do not complain too much about having a wounded soul
The wound burns the lips that touch
It will snow tears like honey in the mouth
Your words will be sweeter with your eyes having been washed

Do not complain too much about your sister death
You will be this Lamb we call Tenderness
Who trembling with love before the knife
Embraces the agony like the child a caress

CHAPTER SEVEN

ACCEPTING TO LET GO

One needs sixty years
to become a man,
and after becoming one,
one needs to prepare to die.
André Malraux

Modern research tends to demonstrate that stages of life exist in the development of adults, stages normal and foreseeable, even though individuals grow in different ways. These are called transitions of life. In a period of transition, sometimes one brings into question problems of the past which were not resolved.

According to Daniel Levinson, a researcher in psychology, a transition "is the end of something, a process of separation or loss." He adds that "the goal of transition is the ending of an era of life and accepting the losses that led to this closing; examining and evaluating the past to decide which aspects of the past will be kept and which will be rejected. One is suspended between the past and the future and wrestles with overcoming the gulf separating them."[78]

Levinson considers the forties as mature age and gives this stage the name "transition in mid-course." For most people, this period,

[78] Daniel J. Levinson, *The Seasons of a Man's Life* (New York: Ballantine Books, 1986).

sometimes extending into the mid-fifties, is one of crisis, mourning, and acceptance.

For most people, in the life of any normal person – laity or priest, religious celibate, married or widowed woman or man – there is, in the course of time, some inevitable period, and I would even say "a relentless age." According to Péguy: "This age does not let itself be deceived. It is not fooled. It does not hide anything. It does not shield us from anything. All is revealed; all betrays us. Forty years old is an unforgiving age because it is the age when we become what we are."[79]

Let us say that between forty and fifty years old is the period of unpleasant discovery: *I am only this; man is only that*, earth and life. It is the manifestation of our limits, the precariousness of our means, the wounds, perhaps shameful, that we have repressed or denied until now, and that *vocation, mine*, may not be realized as I dreamed it, or as described in edifying books from my youth. And Péguy ends with an objective observation, pessimistic perhaps, when he wrote: "The forty-year-old man knows what he knows, and he knows that one is not happy," or at least that true happiness is not the same as thought of in my youth.

Albert Lassus, O.P., writes:

> At one time or another, a man or woman has the painful impression that there is almost evidence of failure within his home, his vocation, his professional activities, his moral life, together with an all-encompassing mediocrity, not to mention even more. They realize their own faults, and even though for a time they have reassured the spirits and hearts of others and inspired great enthusiasm, often everything closes itself too quickly simply to re-enter into banality and tepidness. Then it is not rare that the insidious

[79] Charles Péguy, Oct.23, 1910, *Victor Marie, comte Hugo* (Paris: 1922), 19-22.

visitor that our ancients so dreaded comes knocking:
I mean acedia, the dangerous sadness.[80]

I remember a man in his late forties who, with teary eyes, confessed: "I look behind and only see emptiness." The temptation of letting go, of divorcing life, is then so strong that many yield to it. But it is the time for a new *yes to life*, a time for accepting one's limitations that leads to serenity. But some persons never accept this and drag their life along with some kind of disenchantment: "Now I understand," they tell themselves, bitter and disillusioned.

Many recognize the epilogue of *La force des choses* from Simone de Beauvoir, when, in her fifties, she looks back: "I see the edge of hazel trees jostled by the wind and the promises affecting my distressed heart when I contemplated this gold mine at my feet: a whole life to live. This life has remained. However, looking back with incredulity toward this credulous adolescence, I express with astonishment the extent to which I have been defrauded."[81]

It has been said that Simone de Beauvoir is an unbeliever and that this is probably the reason she speaks this way, but the mid-life crisis and the impression of being "cheated" happens to everyone, including believers, priests, religious, etc.

I believe that many people would not have let go of everything if they had been reassured by being told that this life transition is normal. The teenager with great dreams, the productive young man, has become little by little this man, this adult, who is facing his wounds and his limits. Then, it is natural to think that one made a mistake, one was poorly advised, one should not have married so young, that one did not have a vocation, and subsequently one starts looking, as the saying goes, "on the other side of the fence."

It is both an important and a dangerous moment, like a new physical, psychological and spiritual rebirth. One can say, however,

[80] Albert Lassus, *La vie spirituelle*, No. 560 (Paris: Le Cerf, 1945), 530.
[81] Simone de Beauvoir, *La force des choses* (Paris: Éditions Gallimard, 1963).

that this crisis is not a tragic one; I dare say that this period can be a *blessed time* since we then become ourselves with our wounds and fragility that we must finally accept.

Defrosting

Psychologists, who have attempted to describe the different stages of development of human personality, have concentrated their attention on childhood and the teenage years, and had not focused on this period between thirty-five and fifty-five which appears to be a small element of psychology. In the last twenty years, however, research on this period of life has started to grow. Despite some inevitable differences, these studies have reached the same fundamental conclusion: the existence of a *middle-age crisis* which often leads to personality transformation.

Some psychologists name this crisis the "crisis of limitations." There is a fight in ourselves between the person that we have become with time, and the person who would like to live. Between forty and fifty years old, some persons express this as a *defrosting*, like a river frozen in ice that re-animates with the arrival of spring. We thought that we had achieved our goals, and now we desire to leave and start anew. Gérard Artaud, in his volume, *Se reconnaître soi-même*, on the identity crisis of the adult, expresses it this way:

> To start-over does not necessarily mean to question the fundamental choices that engaged our life in a certain direction, but to express some aspects of our personality that may have been unrecognized by those choices, and to revise modalities of adaptation that have impoverished us. To start again means to attempt anew an exploration of our inner self by opening the still-locked doors and entering the rooms that are dark. It is, however, another task to commit ourselves to this way. It demands much courage on our part.

> We wanted to grow, but were afraid to grow. In this crisis, the first obstacle to overcome is the fear of ourselves.[82]
>
> We need to let go, to accept this fear, and that distresses us. We thought ourselves as being able to count on the power of reason to give significance to our life and, suddenly, in this mid-life transition, reason itself brings emptiness in us. It is as if the child who was, so long ago, wants to live again. We become humiliated, we feel immature with the needs of a child or perhaps of a teenager. In fact, the person between thirty-five and fifty-five struggles and wrestles with problems surprisingly similar to teenagers. Both live an identity crisis. Each, in his way, asks: "Who am I? What do I want to do with my life? What are my true values?"[83]

Françoise Dolto said: "All maturation passes through humiliations." We need agreeing to let go, to entering into our interior. The man who can have the easiest access to his heart and his interior being is the one who is not searching for appearances and is not giving himself the illusion of grandeur by keeping, at all costs, his social image. Gérard Artaud said: "The best example of the human condition is not necessarily the man recognized for his social success; it is the one who has the courage to admit his wounds and interior conflicts."

The first stage of this mid-life transition is the acceptance of one's aging and finitude. "One is not twenty every day," says the song.

[82] Gérard Artaud, *Se connaître soi-même: la crise d'identité de l'adulte* (Montréal: Éditions de l'homme, 1978).

[83] Gail Sheehy analyzed this period of life as the disappearance of youth, the return of the "archaic world of the dead from childhood," and the need to finally end identification with parents. In our forties, "when we need to discover and recognize our dark side, what do we discover? Our egoism, our greed, our jealousy, our fear, our dependence, our passiveness, our aggressiveness." Wouldn't this also be the time for a *new conversion*, for a *purification* of our false virtues and our idealized image? An old Jesuit father once said that the great thirty-day Spiritual Exercises of Saint Ignatius should be lived *around the age of forty*, because our illusions having fallen, we can truly embark with lucidity on the path of true holiness.

One day, we must truly accept that, even if we "still appear young," we are not, and we cannot relive our twenties or thirties.

The Cult of Youth

Our times have seen the beginning of a movement: the cult of youth. Everyone wants to remain young, or at least to appear youthful. One refuses to age.

The present world is fascinated by youth but, at the same time, does not want children and does not believe in life. In fact, the present world is fascinated by youth because, deep down, it is afraid of death and does not know how to face it. One is without hope, believing that he can find happiness in spending money for futilities. Thirty years ago, in some circles, sex seemed to be taboo, but in our days, suffering and death have become taboo. We try, by all means, to distance ourselves from the thought of aging, suffering and dying.

For example, what are the two terms representing security that allow us to forget about death? To *youth* and *money*, can be added *sex* at all costs. This is why, in our society, the expression "mon pauvre vieux" ["my poor old one"][84] is the height of pity, indicating there is, then, no reliance in money ["my poor"], or youth ["old one"]. But we should know that youth and money are false securities, because there is no lack of dead young people or deceased rich people.

The reason our society wants to see the aged set apart is because the image they project is unbearable. It reminds us of our own aging that is to come. In fact, we are so afraid of our own aging and our own death that we reject it in others.

The Bible says: "Do not disregard your own flesh," but your own flesh is yourself weak, suffering, handicapped, old, fragile, wounded and agonizing. It is also all those around us who reveal to us that they are also wounded and aging, and if they are aging, then we too are

[84] Editor translation.

aging, if they die, then we will also die. We do not want to age and we fear death. We can observe the world today. Is not the characteristic of our time the *fear of dying*, and *boredom with living*? We seem to evade this boredom through pleasures, travels, material goods, noise, speed, sex, and even work.

If our contemporaries are unable to accept sufferings, failures, aging and death, it is because they have lost the sense and taste for *Life*. Having rejected the best of their Christian traditions, they are divided between the boredom with life and the fear of aging.

To Accept Aging

Addressing young students, the poet Pierre Emmanuel said one day: "I do not wish you to remain young...I wish you to age, to know how to age."

To succeed in aging and to arrive at a certain serenity, one needs, in some way, to start early and not delay it as long as possible. Accepting to let go, accepting to age, means accepting many renunciations, many losses, and accepting the perspective of death with serenity. Why do so many men and women have great difficulty with the process of aging? I think it is because we all have difficulty accepting the truth and reality of our finitude and mortality.

Henry Nouwen recounts with humor the event that occurred when the community of L'Arche celebrated his sixtieth birthday. John Bloss, a disabled man, who had difficulty expressing himself, was present as a friend of Henry. Someone asked: "John, what can you say to Henry today?" John, who could be somewhat theatrical at times, stood up, placed himself in the middle, and looking straight at Henry, turned red and stammered: "You...You...are..." Everybody was looking at him, wondering what he would say. As he was making efforts to end his sentence, suddenly, in an explosion, the words blurted out like a revelation: "You...You are...old!" Everyone laughed and Nouwen remarked: "Telling me that I have become an old man – very few people would have had the courage to tell me directly on my birthday, and many would have reassured me by telling me that I still looked young and did not show my age; but John, in his truth and simplicity asserted: 'You are becoming old.'"[85]

Generally in our society, we consider persons young until their thirties; between thirty and sixty we consider them in middle-age; those who are over sixty are considered "old" by young people. However, if one attains sixty himself, he does not feel old. To consider oneself old does not come easily, especially in our Western society that glorifies the teenage years and youth. Perhaps we need a prophet like John to tell us clearly and strongly.

Being told that we are old points us toward our aging and our own death. When I was twenty years old, I told myself that I would certainly attain double, and when I was forty, I was not so sure of attaining eighty someday. Now that I am almost sixty, I am certain that I will not attain double and that death is closer to me than the day of my birth. Where are the persons who, like John, have enough simplicity to tell the generations over sixty that they are *old* and need to accept it?

Old...an Insult or a Compliment?

Our modern world has a fear of aging. Innumerable are those who try to not think or talk about it. Close to thirty years ago, was not the expression "the third age" invented to evoke aging more delicately without pronouncing the word? And after the third age came the brilliant idea of speaking of the "golden age"! Someone mentioned to me that, in our religious communities, the expression "old brother" or "old sister" does not exist anymore. We prefer to call them our "seniors," probably thinking of having more respect for them by telling

[85] Henri J M Nouwen, *Our Greatest Gift: a Meditation on Dying and Caring* (New York: Harper San Francisco, 1994).

them that they are not that old. "Should one laugh or cry?" as sung by Jean Ferrat.

If, in the Western world, there are not old people but only persons in the third age, the golden age, or "seniors," by contrast, on the African continent, in the Philippines or India, telling someone that he is old is a compliment and a recognition of his wisdom that can be dispensed to younger generations. In our Western society, lifts, hair grafts and wigs have become the dream of those who desperately reject the aging process.

From Middle-Age to Old Age

In order to enter the third age with serenity, we need to move through this transition of mid-life.

In life, there are two major turning points: the passage from childhood to adulthood that moves through the crisis of adolescence, and the one from adulthood to the wisdom of old age that passes through another crisis, sometimes called "the mid-life crisis." This one, well-lived, should lead us to serenity. It is about letting go, about accepting to age, and accepting with lucidity the perspective of death.

Mid-Life Crisis

Let us try to observe what is happening in the forties through the mid-fifties. The crisis of the forties, that some call the mid-life crisis, happens in the life of an individual between the ages of thirty-five and fifty-five. It is a period of tumultuous interior agitation that sometimes manifests itself in behavior and precedes the advent of true maturity into an advanced age. It can stretch for many years or last for just one: the precise timing or the duration varies among individuals.

There are no clear criteria to determine the beginning of that transition of mid-life. At some point, slowly or suddenly, one realizes that they are not young anymore, that time has passed, and that they have more yesterdays than tomorrows. One measures the distance between the dreams of youth and their effective realization: one might think that the dream followed was not his own, and that a whole aspect of personality has been asleep. Like the thirty-nine-year-old individual in the works of the author Mircea Eliade, one can sometimes say: "You cannot imagine the pain of feeling that time has preceded us, that we have not accomplished some essential projects in the allotted time, that we will wake up one day alone, older, and that nothing can be done. That afternoon, the feeling of the irreparable weighed the heaviest."[86]

Then, it can be said, that each individual discovers himself, not as he has dreamed, but as he is, *a sinner*. As written by Jean Sullivan: "Sooner or later, one needs to remove his mask – at least before himself...Consenting to be oneself is one's intimate poverty, rich or poor, everything lies within."

Coming face-to-face with our limits, and particularly our finitude and our mortality, is also an invitation to another type of relationship with people and things: one learns that control and domination may not have the last word, but one must learn to let go and accept some dispossession.

Carl Jung maintained that the passage from the exterior, in order to carve a place in society – to the interior, in order to find in our selves the answer to questions – is a crucial element for adapting to mature age. It presupposes a period of questioning ulterior motives. This crisis is also closely linked to the consciousness of aging. The first part of adult life is over: one is established in a career or vocation, one has a family or is devoted to some work, project, or community, and is emancipated from their parents. After several years in a career that one has pursued feverishly, a question comes to mind when exploring the interior: "What have I done with my life?"

[86] Mircea Eliade, *Noces au paradis* (Paris: Gallimard, 1981), 239.

One is then led, in a profound way, to facing suppressed problems because one has feared facing them before. The mid-life transition constitutes the most important stage in the cycle of life. According to authors and psychologists, it consists of three essential tasks: re-evaluate the past, modify life's structure, and attain a greater individualization.

In reconsidering his past and his life, the individual needs to acknowledge his future death, and sometimes he lives with a great delusion.

This transition brings us to posing the eternal questions, but now they are founded on our past experiences and the life that we have lived.

"What have I done with my life? What are my true values? Who am I outside of my function, my career, my status? What have I accomplished with the dreams of my youth; what do I want to do with the time left? How does it all harmonize?"

The time has come to grieve one's youth – the time of delusion – and to renew our 'yes' to life, to our vocation, to our spouse, etc. One needs abandonment and to accept aging, to accept sacrificing some dreams of our youth and finally letting go.

Before letting go, however, there is often a journey and even an upheaval ahead. Many persons question themselves in a radical manner.

Adrian Van Kaam expresses it this way:

> Then one says: Should I do something else? Should I act differently? Am I not a prisoner of my marriage, of my vocation? Why continue as before? Opening up to something else, a new start, a new orientation, a new marriage could offer me perhaps some new avenues. It

> is then that the disenchantment of one's life leads to a crisis and a purification of faith. It is at this moment of disenchantment that some religious fall in love for the first time, and that some others – who seemed happy in their marriage – start to think of another man or another woman. During these years of crisis, all the obligations become as oppression.[87]

Is it not in this period that several priests and religious have doubted their vocation and that many couples suddenly saw their marriage shaken? There is a moment of panic because there are more years behind than in front. Some persons who are afraid of this crisis and of letting go may sometimes adopt the behavior of a teenager: going out, drinking, driving fast, taking pills, envying the freedom of the young – even of one's own children – taking dance lessons in order to give themselves the illusion of youth and vitality. One is afraid without mentioning it. All of a sudden, our friends – if not ourselves – start having health problems: cholesterol, angina, cardiac episodes, or the beginning of cancers. Some of them, whom we know well, men and women of our age, are dying. We would like to be reassured and desire to hear someone say: "Do not worry, you will never die." But we know that we have more years behind us than before us. Then we can fall – many do – into depression. In this crisis, we often live an intense period of evaluation. To assess oneself means to open heart and soul to see oneself better. It is not without pain. As a doctor must open parts of the body to extract what is defective, the mid-life person must dive into their depths to see what is not functioning properly.

Some individuals do not want to enter this stage of life. They regress toward a false youth or flee even more into work, pleasure, entertainment or a superficial unbridled sexuality.

[87] See more detail: André Daigneault, "De la crise du milieu de la vie au renouveau du coeur," *Du coeur de pierre au coeur de chair* (Québec: Les Éditions le Renouveau, 1989).—Ed.

Refusing to Age

One desires to remain young at any cost. It is the period when a man would like to purchase a hair piece and a woman thinks of a face-lift. Like a teenager, a person in their forties, and sometimes in the fifties or more, looks for something new, follows trends, amuses themselves, and panics when there is nothing to do. It would be important for them to enter sincerely into their interior, but it frightens them.

"It happens," writes Maurice Bellet, "that the mid-life crisis, undoubtedly known by every human being, at times brings to the surface what is lacking in adolescence. At the age of maturity, men and women with responsibilities, investments, and engagements are waking up from what appears like a strange sleep."[88]

The repressed heart takes its due. In mid-life, we need to reconcile with our childhood, with our heart of a child. Sometimes a mature individual realizes that his fast development did not permit him to build his adult personality on the solid base of an accomplished childhood. He feels in himself the need to walk through some stages in slow motion and relive some experiences of childhood that were uprooted without having savored them sufficiently.

When approaching the mid-life transition, contrary forces may stir up in us a desire to relive childhood, a taste of bursting adolescence and, at the same time, an emptiness, a fear, a feeling of routine, of *déjà vu* and even a weariness of life. Is there something other than this?

A New Yes to Life

In *Les âges de la vie*, Romano Guardini describes this period:

> Then comes the crisis: man feels more clearly the limits of his strength. Work accumulates and solicitations multiply. Over time, one experiences fatigue; one finds that

[88] Maurice Bellet, *Le dieu pervers* (Paris: Le Cerf, 1987).

"it is too much;" one would like to rest; one starts to cut into their reserves, especially when work accumulates to excess, when one is too pressured, when difficulties appear insurmountable.

The illusions disappear and not only those that constitute the essence of youth, but also those that came from the newness of life not yet worn out by experience.

Until then, seriousness, the spirit of decision, the courage to embark, to build and to wrestle has dominated the conscience. All this now loses its newness and freshness, its passionate stimulating character.

The "attraction" of a new meeting, of a new enterprise, is blunted. Existence takes the color of the well-known. There is a feeling of repetition. Routine is felt everywhere.

The poverty of existence is more and more disclosed. One looks behind the scenes and sees that things are more miserable than assumed.

Man is taken over by weariness, a certain distaste for life. In adolescence, one often has the feeling of an eternal promise. It gives man the courage to penetrate into the unknown of life, to assume engagements influenced by friendship, love and the choice of profession.

As life advances, this promise loses strength. The look is penetrating, the heart loses confidence. It is clearer that promises are not always kept, that one reaps less than what was sown. All of this leads to a great disenchantment and a crisis.

The alternative is the following: this disenchantment, this deception, the realization of the poverty of life will dominate, and man can become a skeptic who then performs the necessary tasks in a mechanical way because one needs

> to live; he will harden himself into a forced optimism that he does not feel himself; he will heap work upon work, will elude his family, will try to escape by all means. Or he can say a new *yes* to life, can accept his wounds and his limits. Then a new stage will commence which will be the beginning of wisdom and true maturity. [89]

To Live with Mourning

This type of mourning that we must live with in *mid-life* is often difficult to undertake because it comes from accepting the death of the dreams that we hoped to realize before dying. It is the crucial time (between forty and sixty years old) when we must face our limits whether physical, emotional or psychological. We are now forced to look realistically at what is possible and what is no more, and will never be. Accepting to let go and to lose control is an experience of interior death that we must live and undertake if we desire entering into a happy and serene old age.

We then live a "passage," an "Easter," and an experience of death and resurrection. It is often a difficult period for a couple, a celibate, a religious or a priest. Repressed feelings surface: sadness, distaste, anger, rage, blame of other persons, of a group or our own community that we may have idealized at times.

It is often at this moment that our shell yields and our natural heart starts to live.

Roger Gould writes:

> In order to have an adult sense of freedom, we need to go through periods of passivity, rage, depression and despair, by experiencing the repugnance of death, the tearing of life, the evil in us and around us. To profit from full access to our interior being, we no longer deny the ugly and demonic

[89] Romano Guardini, *Les âges de la vie* (Paris: Éditions du Cerf, 1956.)

side of our life which claims total security is possible, the thought that our immature idea tries to protect by becoming a slave of false illusions.[90]

When these painful feelings appear, it is not a question of denying or repressing them: we need to pass through the night and through tears in order to arrive gently at the serenity of a new day.

Then comes the moment of reconciliation with our life and its limits. The time comes to forgive and be forgiven and to reconcile with our parents, even if they have been deceased for a long time.

Many persons embittered and closed in on themselves suffer in their souls, their hearts and their bodies from a refusal to forgive. Some doctors even say this is a major cause of several illnesses. One needs to know, they affirm, that concealed resentments, sometimes hidden for many years, are "causes of physical or psychological ailments." The current thinking says that the hate and resentments *tormenting* us are wearing us down; they sometimes *undermine* the integrity of our immune system which, according to doctors, can produce serious illnesses. Resentments and the sin not confessed continue their work of interior destruction in weakening our vital strength and sapping our energy; from this comes the necessity (especially for Catholics) for a sincere confession of our faults in the Sacrament of Forgiveness and the importance of reconciling our differences as soon as possible, "before sunset," as mentioned in the Bible.

Serenity comes through reconciliation, acceptance and forgiveness.

Aging Well

The long journey toward serenity is first accepting the unachieved and letting it go. After the mid-life crisis, the long journey toward wisdom begins. Jung speaks of the noon of life which is the beginning

[90] Roger L. Gould, *Transformations: Growth and Change in Adult Life* (New York: Simon and Schuster, 1978), 162.

of descent and of letting go. It is a new chance for a man or woman to interiorize and find themselves apart from their function. In the mid-fifties, a new opportunity is offered to men and women, an opportunity that demands reflection on the meaning of life: will one continue in frenetic work and remain a slave of their old idea that work is the only foundation of their value, or will they interiorize themselves and grow by cultivating other values?

Jung said: "To refuse aging is as foolish as refusing to grow out of childhood." For him, the first part of life is situated in the domain of production, and the second part is more spiritual and meditative. "What youth has found and needed to find in the exterior," writes Jung, "man, in his afternoon, must find inside himself."[91]

This second turning point, expressed by Jung, is not at the point of retirement, in the evening of life, but in mid-life between forty and fifty years old.

"Mid-life," he writes, "is the time of intense expenditure when a person, with all his might and his will, is fully engaged in his works. But it is also the moment of twilight when the second half of life begins... At noon, the descent first begins, overthrowing all the values and ideals of the morning."[92]

Ultimately, to arrive at serenity and succeed in aging, one needs to let go. It is during the forties or at least at the start of the fifties, when one needs to see the importance of interiorizing, reflecting, and organizing one's existence toward a lifestyle which is less productive, but more fruitful, instead of being fully absorbed by a social and professional flurry.

Aging well does not consist of playing golf, traveling, or taking line-dance lessons. Youth does not know what to make of immature, foolish seventy-five-year-olds who play young by showing regression toward a youth that was not sufficiently lived. Our present society

[91] Carl Gustav Jung, *Psychologie de l'inconscient* (Genève: librairie de l'Université, 1952).
[92] Carl Gustav Jung, *Problèmes de l'âme moderne* (Paris: Buchet-Chastel, 1961).

sometimes offers us some strange models of elderly persons who refuse aging and try to retrieve lost time. These persons are not helping the young, quite the contrary. However, one must not generalize because there are also good models.

Many persons in their late sixties are engaged, at their own pace, in volunteer work, taking time for others. They recommit to reading, decide to start painting, study, play a musical instrument, live a more contemplative spirituality, engage with children and youth and therefore, find a new fulfillment and great productiveness. One feels the radiance of these persons that comes from the interior and it brings us some good. Often grandparents can understand their grandchildren better than the parents, receive them and give them the tenderness needed for their development. And what can one say about Christian spiritual values that the elderly offer to their generation? The persons who accept *letting go* and gently accept aging can, without showing it, through their person and their unconditional welcome, evangelize their grandchildren and the youth with whom they come into contact. Without moralizing, they radiate evangelical values through their person or their gentle and kind smile. In this way, an eighteen-year-old youth learned to say the rosary with his grandmother who recited it every day. This youth was proud of having learned it from his grandmother. He, who did not attend Mass, mentioned that he had started saying the rosary before falling asleep. "What is weak in the world," said Saint Paul, "is what God chooses."

To Recover a Meaning to Life

Accepting to let go implies also questioning certain parts of our life. It has been said that in mid-life, men and women need to rediscover their spiritual roots and, sometimes, reconcile with the faith of their childhood that was rejected or set aside. The entry into the transition of mid-life and the beginning of aging must be *a rediscovery of God* and a sincere search for life's meaning. We all know that several psychological and emotional illnesses could have been the result of a lack of love in childhood or of traumatic events. But many of these illnesses can have deeper symptoms. Some depression can be a sign of spiritual deprivation, a feeling of the senselessness of life. At their core, these feelings are essentially repressed or unresolved religious problems.

It appears that, more and more, instead of thinking as before that religion is simply a *tranquilizer* or an escape from reality, psychologists consider it an essential element of mental health. Some psychiatrists still fear religion because of several cases of *mystical delirium* and *religious psychosis* that they have come across. However, one needs to examine if, in cases of *mystical delirium*, there could not be a *false conception* of religion – which I have spoken of in this book – such as negating our *incarnate being*, a search for an ideal *perfection*, contrary to the spirit of mercy that the Doctor of Love came to teach us in the person of Saint Thérèse of the Child Jesus.

All in all, experience proves that a human being cannot live very long by going against the spiritual rules imprinted in himself. He feels more and more empty and seeks the meaning of life in a whirlwind of activity that causes him to never stop in the fear that he will be obliged to reflect on his life. "To fill the void," writes Dr. Artur Janov, "there is never enough alcohol, drugs, clothes or money."

Victor Frankl, an Austrian psychiatrist, says that mental illness, most of the time, should be called *spiritual illness*. He adds: "The effort to find a meaning to life is one of the first motivating forces of man." And when a person is frustrated by this search, in their confusion, they do not always experience mental but *spiritual distress*. In our senior activity centers, do we take seriously, not only the lack of leisure activities for our seniors, but also their *spiritual distress* that, sometimes, hides behind their panic and their efforts to appear young and amuse themselves more and more before dying? Old age and youth sometimes suffer from the same *spiritual distress*. The young from this culture, between fifteen and twenty-five, have one of the highest rates of suicide in the world. Our young people commit suicide and our elders do the same or would like to be euthanized. In our present society, do we heed the *meaning of life*?

Why Am I Living?

In the magazine *Psychiatry*, the Reverend William Brockman, psychologist and pastoral counselor at the American Foundation of Religion, wrote:

> People have recourse to therapy for a number of reasons such as anxiety, loneliness, depression, failed marriage, fear of aging. In fact, what they express is this: "I do not know why I am living; I do not know who I am, and I want to know." They suddenly realize that they have no more goals in life; they have no clear ideas on the meaning of life, of what is important and what is not...Emotionally ill people often have the feeling of nullity. On the surface, many can be charming, spirited, brilliant, but inside themselves is an emptiness and a lack of security. They feel a void and that something is not functioning in them.

A Heart Illness: Absence of Meaning

One can sum up the research of psychologists, overtly Christian and open to spirituality, as follows:

> In its relationship with religion, mental illness can be described at least on two levels: first, as a result of individual alienation from one's intimate spiritual nature (it is the break from God); second, the result of pressures from a materialistic society uniquely focused on the search for excellence that does not account for the human heart and its affective needs, nor for the human soul and its spiritual needs, so this search, then, becomes dehumanizing.

The psychotherapist Victor Frankl also affirms that each era has its particular collective neurosis, and the mass neurosis of our modern age could be called the "spiritual void," meaning that the hectic and materialistic life that we are living makes no sense. "There is a need for adding the soul," as mentioned by Bergson, a philosopher.

Our souls and our consciences are ailing. In his psychiatric study, *The Battle of the Conscience*, Doctor Edmund Bergler disassociates himself from those who consider the conscience as a myth. After treating patients for many years, he now dares to affirm: "Every person has an interior conscience, and the cynic who ridicules the conscience forgets that his own cynicism is not without relating to his own conscience, and that his shameless behavior is only a defensive expression against his internal enemy. He attacks others in order to strike himself." [93]

Letting Go and Rediscovering the True Face of God

Doctor C.G. Jung, who disassociated from Freud at some point, writes:

> In the last thirty years, people from all the civilized countries have come to consult with me. I have treated several hundred patients. Among all my patients over thirty-five, there was no one whose problem was, in the end, not finding a religious perspective in his life. It is fair to say that each one felt ill because he lost what the religions of all ages have given to their followers, and none was truly healed who had not recovered his religious belief.[94]

Doctor J.A. Hadfield, one of the greatest English psychiatrists, wrote long ago: "As psychotherapist, and as such, without relating with theology, I am now convinced that the Christian religion is one

[93] Edmund Bergler, *The Battle of the Conscience: A Psychiatric Study of the Inner Working of the Conscience* (Washington, D.C.: Washington Institute of Medicine, 1948)

[94] Carl Gustav Jung, trans. WS Dell and Carey F. Baynes, *Modern Man in Search of a Soul* (New York: Harcourt Brace World, 1962).

of the most valuable and powerful influences for generating peace of spirit and confidence in the soul, which is necessary to heal a great number of nervously ill patients."

There can be no serene and happy aging without abandonment of prejudices, without reconciliation with the past, and without the rediscovery of one's faith and the true face of God.

I think that, in this long journey toward serenity, we need to let go and accept the renewal of our spiritual values; accept that "to be" is more important than "to do," and that our life has meaning, death has meaning, and that we are really the children of God whom God wanted us to be from all eternity – this God who is Our Father, and also the ultimate answer to the reason for being created.

I Get Used to It

I get used to it
I get used to it slowly
Do not worry too much
I get used to it I get used to it
I barely have a tear in my eye
Barely a slight heartbeat
I get used to falling hair
To my eyes that droop
I get used to it slowly
To less strong light
I walk more slowly
Much more slowly
Do not worry too much
My heart beats harder
Faster
I get used to it slowly
I slowly let go
Of the masks that hid me
I uncover myself slowly
I barely have a tear in my eye
Barely a light sob
My heart of stone softens
My heart of flesh is there

Under my shell
Slowly I show it
Slowly the adornments fall
And here I am fragile
Standing in front of you
Tenderness flowing
From the wound
Of my heart of a child

CHAPTER EIGHT

ACCEPTING TO DESCEND INTO OUR HEART

Return to your heart.

Saint Augustine

Due to scientific progress, the span of human life is increasing unceasingly and one understands that the problems of seniors are very current today, be it physical, economic, or social issues. One speaks often of the activities for retired persons: leisure activities of all kinds, manual activities, dance, sports, trips...without ever, or almost never, the mention of their *interior* and *spiritual* life, their life of *prayer* – in other words – the *essential*.

However, is retirement with its leisure, its apparent freedom, not the privileged period among all, that brings men and women of today, liberated from their burdensome daily labors, a wonderful chance to finally discover the divine dimension of their being, this dimension which was perhaps not accessible until now? The essential questions must be asked: "What is the meaning of your life? Where do you come from? Where are you going? Have you never heard inside yourself the interior voice that is calling and whispers like spring water, 'Come to the Father!'?" [95]

[95] See "Et si l'automne de nos vies pouvaient être vécu comme un nouveau printemps," *Feu et lumière*, No. 79 (1983).

We should not wait until the very end of our life to open ourselves to interiority and spiritual life. Toward the end of the mid-life crisis, there should be a return to the heart and to interiority. Every age has its joys and sufferings, each stage of our life has its particular song. After rejecting the faith and religious practices of their childhood, how many persons have returned, after a trial that led them to their wound, and recognized the thirst of their heart? When the sun sets in the summer of our lives, another song rises up. And in the canticle of our human seasons, the song of our autumns can be beautiful and tender as it prepares us to enter winter. A song of dead leaves?...would it not rather be a song of tenderness and interior life which resembles a fire in the fireplace where it is good to come closer in order to bathe in its glowing and pleasant heat? The forties and fifties are the preparation for a serene old age. "They shall bear fruit even in old age" (Ps 92:15).

Aging is a time to grow and increase in Love, a time to recover our heart of a child. I believe that the autumn of life and old age should be times of mercy and contemplation. It is the age of abandonment, of listening, and of generosity. In his old age, Moses could only extend his arms and pray. In this way, he gave victory to the younger ones who were fighting. There are in us a Martha and a Mary who have their role to play in our lives.

The Gospel speaks to us of these two women who live in intimacy with Jesus but are of different temperaments: *Martha and Mary.* Could we not consider them as the two stages before and after the mid-life crisis? Martha could represent the first part of our life, where engagement and *doing* occupy first place. And then the noon of life arrives. Mary would like to take her place in leading us to the depths of our heart. As Saint Augustine said so well: "You were within me, but I was outside, and it was there that I searched for you."

In his homilies as in his *Confessions,* Saint Augustine more than once invites his listeners or readers to return to their own heart. For Augustine, the heart of man is his "secret room," his "interior mansion." For him, the heart is *par excellence* "the location where God is discovered and tasted." Even the depth of the heart demonstrates that it is "made for God," and this, whether man is conscious of it or not. Only God can fill our heart. This is the meaning of the well-known phrase in the *Confessions*: "You have made us for yourself and our heart is restless until it rests in you."

Augustine is close to the mentality of our contemporaries. "I no longer found myself...I was far away from myself," he said.

From Doing to Being

Carl Jung insists on the approach of reality through the "heart." To love is for the mystic and love is not a concept: it can only be lived. However, the spirit of competition often directs all our activity. We desire to do things; we think of being recognized through our deeds. We have lost the wonder of our heart of a child that enjoys life and simple reality with a curiosity that allows us to be present, rather than desiring to always *do* something.

The long journey toward serenity must lead us from doing to *being*, from producing to fruitfulness, and from giving to receiving. Even from the spiritual point of view, we must learn to let ourselves be loved and let ourselves be.

Man has a heart and he is called to know his heart. God lives in the heart of man: "[The Word] is something very near to you, already in your mouths and in your hearts" (Dt 30:14).

One cannot know someone without grasping the inclination of his heart: "For where your treasure is, there also will your heart be" (Lk 12:34). It is the man without a mask and without a facade whom God wants to meet, the man as God sees him: "God knows our hearts." God probes the heart of man: "He scrutinizes them, the One who scrutinizes the depth of man, the depth of his heart."

In this long journey toward serenity, we need to descend into our heart to meet the One who loves us the way we are. God loves us and sees us as we are. There is no hiding from him. The heart of God is, at the same time, both love and truth. Therefore, we must enter into our heart and accept ourselves with mercy by offering ourselves to Love. The look of the heart that God offers is a look of love. We cannot see ourselves in truth without seeing ourselves with love. When we have accepted to acknowledge ourselves as sinners, we must recognize this wounded child in ourselves and see him with love and truth. Whatever we have done, whatever our pride, our pharisaism, we must, after admitting it to ourselves, let ourselves be forgiven and forgive ourselves. Surely it is good to have lived in truth, but we must never forget that truth without love is not truth: it is demeaning, hurtful and ultimately sterile; truth in love is a source of conversion, fulfillment and bears fruit.

Meeting God in Ourselves

God awaits us in the depths of our heart. We need to descend into it. As mentioned by Elizabeth of the Trinity: "It seems to me that I have found my heaven on earth, since heaven is God, and God is in my soul. The day that I understood this, everything was illuminated in me and I would like to share this secret gently to all whom I love."

The more we age, the more we desire to discover the importance of the prayer of the heart and prayer in our life. From our fifties, we need to discover a contemplative sense of life and prayer of the heart because, without this, we experience catastrophes and maybe even a total collapse.

Jean Lafrance writes:

> I must say, that around forty years old, I entered a period of great turmoil; it lasted more than a dozen years. It is then that I discovered the prayer of supplication. One word ended this period of turbulence: "I will heal you through prayer and only through prayer." I cannot declare the origin of this word. What is certain is that, progressively

> and even rapidly, I entered into a much calmer and more peaceful era. [96]

One would not be able to gain ground toward peace of heart without going through the necessity of interiority and entrance into the depths of our heart.

Saint John of the Cross calls the heart "the center of the soul" and he also says: "This center of the soul is God." He adds: "Health of the soul is God's love."

Some people refuse to enter into their interiority. They continue to live on the surface of themselves and remain immature and superficial, unfortunately until their death. This message of Saint Augustine – returning to the center of ourselves, descending to the depths of our heart to reach God, and discovering the truth of our being – is also the one from Bernanos, who six months before his death, in the last pages of his journal, wrote these few lines: "We desire all that He wants, but we do not know that we want it, we do not know ourselves, sin makes us live on the surface of ourselves, we will enter into ourselves only to die, and this is where He waits for us."[97] Without totally contradicting Bernanos, I dare to hope that many will enter into themselves and descend into their heart *before* their death. The holy Curé of Ars said: "Interior life is like a bath of love into which the soul plunges." And Thérèse of Lisieux added: "I understand and know by experience that the Reign of God is inside of us." I sincerely believe that prayer can be of help in the physical and mental health of a human being.

God and the Psychiatrist

In a surprising and, at the same time, overwhelming volume, Doctor Balthazar Stähelin, a German psychiatrist, affirms: "One must associate psychotherapy and the revelation of Christian faith because the spirit

[96] Jean Lafrance, *Jour et nuit* (Montréal: Éditions Mediaspaul, 1992), 8.
[97] Albert Béguin, *Bernanos par lui-même: dernier agenda, Tunisie, 24 Janvier 1948* (Paris: Éditions du Seuil, 1954), 147.

of Christ is in everyone's psyche." It is not an insignificant person who says this, but a medical psychiatrist and consultant in psychosomatic medicine at the medical polyclinic of the University of Zurich:

> In our times, the first question is formulated this way: Is the revelation of the Trinity that reaches each human individual authentic and real? My personal response as a therapist is a firm yes.
>
> The basic idea and the centerpiece of my therapy is to reconnect the link between the temporal and the spiritual, between temporal reality and the spirit of the triune God of Christians or, during therapy, to at least reinforce their capacity to believe it.
>
> The break between the human being and God, from which comes anxiety and illness, must be abolished. The human being was created and endowed with a psychosomatic disposition to receive God, to carry him, and to respond to his love.
>
> Today, most of us will say that there is a need to learn to pray again. For myself, as a therapist and psychiatrist for more than thirty years, I am not afraid to affirm that prayer remains the most important task to save humanity. We need to let ourselves be loved and embraced in faith, we need to surrender and love in the context of this presence in us that is the Trinity.[98]

And, in a conference given about health, Doctor Stähelin said:

> The end of our millennium is characterized by an increase of trouble and psychic illnesses because materialism has invalidated the universal conception, accepted up to now, of the presence of a supernatural God working in each individual.

[98] Balthazar Stähelin, *L'Inconscient marial: guide médical de cheminement vers Dieu* (Montréal: Bellarmin, 1985).

It is why we must, in work and leisure, strive to recover the triune God as a fundamental value. In order to find and deepen one's faith, we must learn to pray an hour a day, month after month, for all of our life. He proposes four basic principles of psychosomatic therapy to find peace and interior serenity:

· Every night, before falling asleep, read for a half-hour a few pages from the Bible or some spiritual reading and try to harmonize the reading with one's own life.

· Rise early in the morning, start with listening to some classical or religious music, and dedicate a half-hour to bodily relaxation through exercise (bicycling, gymnastics, jogging, etc.).

· After physical exercise, abandon oneself in silence, entering one's heart and the prayer of the heart in the most total physical or psychic inactivity, a time of personal or mental prayer.

· Finally, during the day, try entering into one's heart, interiorize and live the Divine Presence in one's soul.

And Doctor Stähelin observes that, after a while, sometimes a dramatic transformation can occur in terms of serenity and deep peace. The person is no longer the same and radiates kindness and love.

The Need for Interiority

Our world is more and more thirsty to find a fruitful inner life. "This world needs interiority more than ever. Every moment of human life seems to be disordered by the search for accomplishments, for entertainment, or for the noisy voice of the media. But man also needs some prolonged silence and free contemplation" (John Paul II, January 22, 1987). [Saint] Pope John Paul II did not hesitate to invite bishops and priests to lead *themselves first* by an intense prayer life in order to lead others after them. "At the moment of our episcopal ordination, the consecrating bishop asked us: 'Do you want to pray without ceasing for the people of God and fulfill, as it should, the sacerdotal function of a bishop?' But how to raise up masters of prayer? How to train Christian people to pray better themselves?"

"More people than we believe would be able to pray from the heart," added John Paul II, "but no one has taught them. Without this interiority, the Baptized run out of steam, their action becomes a loud cymbal, and even their religious practice, if it exists, is drying up" (February 24, 1982).

It is sad to see many efforts to provide seniors leisure and dance, or to disguise them as witches or jesters for Halloween, while their soul is dying of thirst. It is sad to the point of tears.

Desire for Interior Life

Despite the fascination created by consuming goods, especially in the Western world, a desire of another dimension manifests itself more and more in many people, a desire for a dimension that is more interior and contemplative. "Holiness," says Jean Lafrance, "is not to improve oneself, to become somebody, but to allow the life of Another to penetrate us. It is He who desires us and wants to love us." As Olivier Clement has said: "Open the door of your heart to the beggar who knocks!"

We must accept to descend into our heart and let ourselves be transformed by the fire of God's love.

Wasting Time

The mature age should become a time of interior mental prayer, simplified prayer, and contemplation.

This prayer is not that difficult; it is about wasting time with God, in love. Saint Teresa of Avila has said: "In mental prayer, what is important is not to think much but to love much." Mental prayer is not reserved for intellectuals nor the religious and priests; it is accessible to little ones, the simple, the wounded of heart, the elderly. Perhaps we have complicated mental prayer. How many very simple persons, grandmothers, workers, young persons wounded by life, have arrived at a union of love with God simply by the repetition of the *Hail Mary* in the Rosary? Saint Teresa of Avila affirms that *vocal* prayer can lead us to infused contemplation.

In his volume, *Le chapelet, un chemin vers la prière continuelle*, Jean Lafrance gives us the example of a missionary who practiced *the prayer of the heart* for many years and, at the end of his life, turned to the Rosary as a means of mental prayer:

> I feel that I now must take the "Hail Mary" as personal mental prayer in order to pray unceasingly. I had the intuition that I needed to repeat the second part of the prayer. Am I ready to adopt the Rosary permanently during my mental prayer? I wish it and I desire it. I feel the need to unify my whole prayer; at this moment, I try to remain with the Rosary during the time of my mental prayer and the "Hail Mary" for the rest of the day.[99]

Here we have the testimony of a missionary who became so simple that he actualized his mental prayer with the Rosary by using the *Ave* as a prayer of the heart based on the model of the "Jesus prayer." At the end of his life, he embraced in his heart the simplicity of an old grandmother who constantly fingers her Rosary, repeating the Hail Mary, radiating peace and serenity.

Many very old persons that we believe to be completely senile, calm down and are pacified when we recite the Rosary with them. There is something mysterious in this which should make us think.

[99] Jean Lafrance, *Le chapelet : un cheminement vers la prière continuelle* (Montréal: Éditions Mediaspaul, 1987), 39.

Toward Serenity

Our world needs men and women of prayer. Playing golf, bowling, constantly traveling, playing cards, or taking dance lessons is not evil in itself, but I believe that the human heart is made for *more* than this. We need to descend into our hearts, to enter into ourselves to rediscover the presence of God that dwells in us. "In you," said Saint Augustine, "there is someone greater than you."

The present generation, youth and elderly, are searching for *masters of prayer*. Some years ago, one encountered suicide mainly among the young, but now we are increasingly worried in the face of an upsurge in attempts of suicide by the elderly. The time of contemplation, of some serenity, becomes instead a time of desperation. There is an urgency to help support a rediscovery of the role of deep prayer and mental prayer for the elderly. The long journey toward serenity must go through the rediscovery of God living in us.

I Am Going Now

I am going now to the depth of my tears
Everything will end one day in the pure water of the heart
For so long Love has been calling me
For so long the flowers have been half-opened

I am going now like a snowflake
That shatters in the too hot sun of a summer too hot
For so long my soul has been healing
For so long has it been looking for the Beloved

I am going now naked and unarmed
I take the narrow path that leads me to happiness
And as the pure child prays through his tears
I am going now to the God of my heart

CHAPTER NINE

AGREEING TO RECOVER ONE'S HEART OF A CHILD

The more we age,
the more we discover our own childhood,
and the only way to save ourselves
is to recover the child in ourselves.

Volker Schlöndorff

"The one who has never lost his heart of a child is truly a great man," said Gilbert Cesbron, and for the one who has lost it along the way, it remains to find it someday. Life is altogether beautiful and strange. From a physical point of view, we start by being a child, and youth is the summit. The young person is flexible, agile and strong. But, as we age, we become more rigid, less agile, less strong. From the spiritual point of view, would not the contrary be true? We start out old, slow and rigid, with a heart of stone. But the path of life gradually teaches us to become softened. It is about recovering our heart of a child. The healthiest, the most emotionally balanced adults, are not the ones who appear strong and rational but, on the contrary, are those closest to their childhood; they no longer play a character, they are not stilted, they no longer pretend, they express themselves spontaneously. One feels that we can be ourselves in front of them and that their childlike spirit and their simplicity is not childish regression but rather wonderment for life and creatures. These persons accept themselves with their wounds; they can be close to young people while remaining themselves. The struggle of rediscovering childhood is not always easy. "It takes a long time to become young," said Picasso.

The long journey toward serenity must lead us to a recovered childhood. Let us not fool ourselves, however; the task is far from easy, the path is narrow and strewn with pitfalls. During this long journey, there will be nights to pass through, deserts to cross, and trials to overcome before arriving at this childlike heart.

We do not attain maturity, serenity, and a natural heart without having encountered evil, meanness, rejection, incomprehension, or at least much littleness and wickedness...and these not only from others! Discovering your wounds and your own sin does not come without suffering. The new childhood is always born from reconciliation with the past. We are all creatures of flesh, wounded and sinful. The Virgin Mary alone, having been granted this grace from the beginning, has not lost her original purity, her original childhood. Therefore, Bernanos rightly says: "The gaze of the Virgin is the only true childlike gaze, the only child's gaze that has ever uplifted our shame and our unhappiness."[100] The others, even the saints, had to struggle to recover this first grace, this freshness from the beginning: going from the innocence of before to the innocence of after, which alone deserves the name spiritual childhood and evangelical simplicity.

An Adult with the Heart of a Child

All the saints have actualized in themselves that balance, so effective and so meaningful, between the adult soul and the heart of a child. "The adult," Saint John Chrysostom rightly said, "will not be truly an adult if he is not a child at the same time." In strong and simple terms,

[100] Georges Bernanos, *Journal d'un curé de campagne* (Paris: Plon, 1936).

[Saint] Pope Paul VI quoted: "Becoming a child again means putting back into the mind the native sense of a human creature, the power to learn once again, to wonder, cry, smile and love."[101] It is really to remove your masks and become, at its most authentic, what you are wearing deep down inside yourself. It is finally shedding our persona.

We are not far from the truth by saying it is a question of finding the freshness of a child's gaze, his capacity of wonderment, his fantasy, his non-conformity, the relaxation that we feel in Saint Philippe Neri, Saint John Bosco, and the child that Saint Francis of Assisi was in front of the dignitaries of the Church. Basically, the gaze of a child, the gaze of the old person who has reached serenity and abandonment, and the gaze of the saint have something in common: a certain light, a painful sweetness, a peace that radiates and disarms us.

Having recovered the heart of a child, there is in a man or woman, and in the saint, a simplicity, a non-conformity, a certain naivety and a wonder that sometimes confuse us. The world cannot always tolerate a totally transparent person because it knows that this person cannot be manipulated. There is something disconcerting about someone who has found his heart of a child, like the heart of a saint.

According to the philosopher Aristotle, the saint is the one who keeps intact – or who regains – his power to wonder. The fresh outlook he casts on the world and on people allows him to recognize, beyond the wounds, faults and apparent decrepitude, the forever young God who manifests himself there. Like a child and an old person with a child's heart, he retains the capacity to be astonished and to marvel.

The entrance into old age can be a rediscovery of our deepest heart that we have protected and hidden under our shell of an active and strong man or woman for so many years. This is why only the saints attain, by the way of childhood, true Christian maturity, because we can become transparent only by making ourselves very little. "Once out of childhood," said Bernanos, "it takes a long time of suffering

[101] Daniel Ange, *Paul VI: Un regard prophétique* (Paris: Éditions Saint-Paul, 1979).

to return to it, just as at the end of the night we find dawn." And he added: "I will only be able to regain childhood through holiness."

With the Eyes of a Child

Have you noticed the look of some elderly? It is the look of a child, and the light of God passes through them with a sweetness that comes to seek us in the depths of our heart.

At one time, Jesus was in the presence of Jairus' little girl who died at the age of twelve. Do you know how Jesus brought her back to life? "He entered the room where the child was" (Mk 5:40). If each one of us could enter where the child is in our own heart, the child in our father or mother's heart, the child in our grandfather or grandmother's heart, the child in our child's heart, we would see what is asleep waking up, what is lifeless reviving, what is dead resuscitating.

Old age, childhood, and youth are close to one another. For example, why do grandparents often find it so easy to come into contact with their grandchildren? It is that they themselves have found their heart to be as vulnerable as a child. They don't play grown-up anymore. Life has made them so simple and vulnerable that they are closer to the fragility of each human being. And the young people don't need to arm themselves defensively against them. Meanwhile, often young people feel misunderstood by their own parents who are in their prime, who are wearing shells and defenses.

To Let the Child Live

The child, the elderly, the saint, these three are joined in their trust and their simplicity. They are completely themselves without masks or defenses. During their entire life, some people hide their fragility under a shell. They appear strong and rational, nevertheless are the most fragile of creatures. One realizes, at times, that these persons are unable to become childlike again because they have never lived a true childhood.

How many children have never been themselves? Certain parents have pressured their child by attributing to them the role of being what they themselves would have liked to have become, and even to becoming the *glory of the family*.

The analyst, Peter Lomas says:

> We have a tendency to believe that the sense of identity unfolds precisely...from the attribution of a defined role in the family system. But there is a noticeable difference between recognizing the other as a unique human being and recognizing his uniqueness in his role. When parents impose on a child a role that does not take into consideration who he truly is, the result can be disastrous. They steal his childhood and his life.

If you have seen or read the theater play, *The Death of a Salesman* by Arthur Miller,[102] you might remember the character of Biff Loman, the son of Willy. This forever teenager is unable to find his life. And if he is unable, it is because he is a prisoner of the role imposed by his father. At thirty-four years old, raging, and in pain, he explodes in a scene perhaps more overwhelming than the play: "I am not a leader of men, Willy, and neither are you...I'm one dollar an hour, Willy! I tried seven states and couldn't raise it...Do you gather my meaning?" His father refuses to hear him and Biff continues, screaming: "Pop, I'm nothing! I'm nothing, Pop. Can't you understand that...I'm just what I am, that's all."

Willy continues to not listen. He has projected his dreams onto his sons. Empty of his fury, Biff collapses at this father's feet, sobbing in a last attempt at genuine communication with him: "Will you let me go, for Christ's sake? Will you take that phony dream and burn it before something happens?" But Willy prefers to die rather than

[102] Arthur Miller, Eric Kahane, *La mort d'un commis voyageur: conversation privée en deux actes et un requiem* (Paris: L'Avant-Scène, 1966); Arthur Miller, *Death of a Salesman: Conversations in two acts and a requiem* (London, England: Peguin Books, 1961).

accept reality. His sons don't know what they are. They did not have a true childhood and, inside their manly bodies, hides a *wounded child* who would like so much to be loved for himself. This theater play is a real therapy for some men who have had no childhood and have played a role all their life.

In his volume, *La société sans père*, Alexandre de Willebois explains what happens to children who have no childhood and who have been forced to become adults too quickly:

> A child who is constantly presented with a truncated self-image, a child on whom a role is imposed too early and from whom we expect results that he cannot provide, a child who is forced too soon to become adult, such a child may be overwhelmed with feelings of inferiority and develop an unconscious self-hatred.
>
> In order to valorize himself, he might choose to rid himself of his real self and, at a more advanced age, search to affirm himself through a borrowed personality, meaning a facade of a pseudo spectacular personality through which he tries to compel the admiration of others. It is then a narcissistic solution, a search for glory.[103]

His lack of love is hidden under a false self-assuredness. Karen Horney speaks to us of the wounded personality that is hiding within himself. "In his projects and activities, he exalts and cultivates everything that leads him to control. The domination of others manifests itself by the need to perceive himself superior. He has an inability to maintain equal relationships. Such a person must be in charge, otherwise he sees himself completely lost and helpless."

Basically, when Saint Paul affirms: "It is when I am weak that I am strong," he wants to also affirm that it is sometimes the creature that seems the weakest, the most fragile – who knows it, and accepts

[103] Alexandre de Willebois; Annick Bogaert; Jacques de Bourbon Busset, *La société sans père: enquête psychoculturelle sur la civilisation sécularisée* (Paris: S.O.S., 1985).

it – who can go through certain trials without a breakdown; on the other hand, a serious person, who gives the appearance of strength, can collapse to the surprise of many. False strength is weakness, and true weakness becomes strength. This is the human and evangelical paradox. Accepted weakness and recovered childhood become factors of interior strength and human maturity. In fact, the one who has found his heart of a child is unafraid to be known in his weakness. Having removed his mask, he gives hope to others to remove theirs. Little by little, on this long journey toward serenity, we come to accept ourselves as we are, with our weaknesses. We finally stop playing a character and we move toward spiritual maturity through rediscovered childhood.

Toward a New Simplicity

One of the charms of childhood is its unabashed spontaneity. The child is simply himself. It is said that truth comes out of the mouth of children. "All who heard him were astonished by his intelligence and his answers," was spoken of the Child *par excellence*. Unfortunately, this period of simplicity does not last. It is lost in the teenage years when masks replace simplicity of heart. The adult loses in simplicity and spontaneity what he gains in independence. Useful occupations and concerns that monopolize the adult, to the benefit of action and commitments, restrict his free time and the possibility of opening his heart and listening. After the fifties, and at the end of the mid-life transition, a descent begins into a new childhood of the heart. For that, we need to accept abandoning ourselves, and not desiring to control anything. The end of role-playing can be the end of the personas, and the rediscovery of our heart of a child which emerges with the fall of our masks. Retired from business, from work, the older individual is less tempted to bluff and play a character. He has nothing to lose, he can finally become himself. As he feels the hour of truth approaching – which no one escapes – appearances and what will be said about him lose importance in his eyes. Free from smugness and self-sufficiency, impoverished by false wealth, his personality is reduced more and more to the deep truth of his being. So long repressed, his heart of a child finally reappears and the eyes light up and soften. The wonder of a child appears at the same time as abandonment and the acceptance of receiving, and of allowing himself to be truly loved in his smallness. And through denudation and impoverishment, God reveals himself in a new simplicity. The heart is made like that of God, more merciful. Through the purgatory of sufferings and denudation, old age is a deep call to a more contemplative life. It is the time of hope and abandonment.

The more we age, the more we realize that humility is not what we have thought. "I give praise to you, Father, Lord of heaven and earth, for though you have hidden these things from the wise and the learned you have revealed them to the childlike" (Mt 11:25). "These things" being precisely the face of God who is the face of meekness and disarming childhood. Jesus does not say "the stupid" but *the little ones* who, at the same time, become the most intelligent. True intelligence, which is to be distinguished from all intellectualisms, is the candor of a child's gaze that penetrates the depth of things. Is this not the intelligence of the heart that we must find as we age? When the active man and woman are glued to their possessions or behind the mask of their persona, they no longer really know who they are, and *to appear* "kills" the *to be*. However, sooner or later, through the trials of life or illnesses, we need to face the essential question: "What meaning does my life have? Who am I really?" It is then that we must recognize, lucidly, that our "external self" is not our "true self" and that it is covered by an illusory shell or mask.

Saint John of the Cross speaks of "the night of the senses and of the soul" that we must go through to enter the sweetness of the true light beyond the darkness. We prepare ourselves for the great meeting with God who, in truth, will overturn our misconceptions.

As we age, we must move from a heart of stone to a natural heart. Little by little, our heart, softened and impoverished, must not offer any resistance to the invasion of Love. During his conversion, André Frossard met with God who transformed his life. In his volume, *Il y a un autre monde*, he relates this encounter with the eternal childhood of God:

> I have learned that he is gentle, a gentleness unlike any other, which is not the passive quality sometimes referred to by this name, but an active, shattering sweetness surpassing all violence, capable of bursting the hardest stone and, harder than stone, the human heart...It is not the omnipotence of God that threatens us, nor what is called his glory, it is his heartbreaking gentleness. It is the eternal and limpid innocence of God that breaks our heart. It cannot be present without us passing judgement on ourselves. And that's what he doesn't want. Everything has in it its reason for charity.[104]

Paul Claudel himself declared that, during his conversion, he met the "heartbreaking and eternal childness of God." Is not all-powerfulness beyond "all weakness" and heartbreaking innocence? Why then, do the eyes of a child move us so much? Is there not in this regard something of the purity, the meekness, and the innocence of God which touches and disarms us beneath our shells? Sometimes meeting the gaze of an old man who has found his heart of a child has the same effect on us. The path to serenity is slow. It is a matter of conversion, of becoming poor, becoming a child to whom are revealed the secrets of the Kingdom. To become a child again we have to abandon ourselves. The long journey toward serenity must pass through surrender and regained confidence. We do not suspect how unaccustomed we are to trusting. We so greatly desire to control our life and, at times, the lives of others. "It is confidence," said Thérèse of the Child Jesus, "and only confidence that brings us to love. Only confidence."

[104] André Frossard, *Il y a un autre monde* (Paris: Fayard, 1976).

The essence of trust is to not look for anything else and to not rely on anything other than love and mercy. Before arriving at this confidence and this abandonment, we cross several deserts. Before entering the serenity of old age, we must go through the dreaded ordeal of the mid-life transition. In this we experience our misery by descending to the depth of our distress. We thought ourselves generous, humble, helpful, of pure intentions, and here we are, realizing with fear that pride is there inside us, right down to our deepest roots. Our apostolic life, our human relations, are mixed with impurities. Before the serenity of the third age, we come face to face with our sin. We are truly "like the rest of humanity." It is a time of the noonday demon, but it is also the time for abandonment and a new conversion. We have a new choice to make. We discover that we are inhabited by sin: "True, I was born guilty, a sinner, even as my mother conceived me" (Ps 51:7). Then arrives the time of great mercy and the entry into a new childhood of the heart. At the beginning of our spiritual life, we seek mainly to love God; in the end, we understand that it suffices to let ourselves be loved by him. Like children, we must now offer ourselves to love. In short, we must let God love himself in us. We have to let ourselves be transformed and our heart melted. "The heart of saints is liquefied," stated the Curé of Ars magnificently.

Becoming a child again means accepting to have your heart crushed by the heartbreaking sweetness of love and to drown in the Ocean of Mercy. The saint has regained his heart of a child, and that is why he is no longer afraid of God because he has consented to let himself be immersed in the Ocean of Love, to let himself be carried away by the gentleness of Divine Mercy. Isn't this the journey that we have to travel to reach the threshold of the third age, toward the serenity which, unbeknown to us, will radiate the clarity and gentleness of God through our being, invaded by the light of eternal childhood?

To Depart I Will Wear

I will wear my best clothes to depart
My sweetest smile my warmest tears
I will wear the light in my eyes to depart
To open my heart to you like a child at play

I will wear my best clothes to depart
And you will not know I am leaving in the morning
You will say he is this child full of life
And in front of my cold body resting on the leaves
You will all find yourselves crying softly

CHAPTER TEN

ACCEPTING TO DIE

Accepting to let go,
accepting to grow old,
but still continuing to love, despite everything.
It is then with serenity,
we can accept to die in peace.

Paul Tournier

In each stage, life offers us different types of learning through whatever we experience. The passage from one stage to another is not without suffering. "There is no love from which we are not bruised," said the poet Aragon. Each step brings its crisis and its mourning to live. So it is the same for this step which leads us to the process that we call *dying.*

Saint Augustine affirms:

> When a human being is born, there are many assumptions: perhaps he will be beautiful, perhaps he will be plain; perhaps he will be rich, perhaps he will be poor; perhaps he will have a long life, perhaps not...But it can be said of no one: perhaps he will die, perhaps he will not die. Death is the only absolutely sure thing in life. What difference

does it make whether it takes a little longer or a little shorter time?[105]

Death is simultaneously the most certain and the most uncertain thing. What is quite certain is the *fact* that it will happen; what is uncertain is the *moment* when it will happen. At each instant of our lives, we experience, under different forms, this act of *dying*. We need detachment. All these changes, the mourning we must endure, will lead us gradually to dispossession from both family and friends: to be pulled out from an environment, to have to change a relationship, to renounce a certain function. All these events can make us grow or close us in on ourselves. We have a choice.

My Life: A Paschal Mystery

Death is present in my life through all the failures that I have experienced, all the illusions that I have entertained, the defeats that have thwarted my will. Time passes that I cannot get back and constantly reminds me that a limit is fixed for my present activity. To exist as a person and to live requires multiple renunciations and disappropriations, while all withdrawal into myself, all tension over my past, over my wealth, all vain bitterness over what could have been, risk preventing me from living and becoming more. My life is a Paschal Mystery of death and resurrection, losses and gains, of living and dying. This constant movement from death to life, from loss of possessing to victory of *being*, from disappropriation to attainment of personhood, imposes itself, it seems to me, as the law of personal existence. This is why, each time I consider the eventuality of my death, in whatever manner I still am not aware of, and that I consent to this death by continuing with my previous choices – which must give new birth to

[105] Saint Augustine, *Confessions* Tome II, livre IX-XIII (Paris: Société d'édition Les belles lettres, 1954), 33.

the creature that I am in the hands of a Father who invites me to love him – I deliberately achieve my vocation as a son or daughter of the Father like Jesus Christ, his firstborn Son. "I lay down my life in order to take it up again" (Jn 10:17).

Death is the opportunity to take off all the masks. This is the real challenge that is offered to me: in the last act of my earthly life, will I identify as the one who, so often, gave himself the illusion of playing his persona alone, and acquiring alone and by himself his earthly securities?...Will I remain a prisoner of my "idealized image" and lock myself in my *ego*? Or, will I finally become who I am? Will I, like Christ, recognize my true personality as this child of God that I am, who is returning to his Father – who perhaps returns from afar at a painful but willingly accepted cost – leaving behind all his attempts to be admired, to play hard, and to pose in front of God as an independent subject? A choice is given to me: to refuse to abandon myself and to harden myself or, by asking forgiveness, to throw myself into the arms of the Father in a final act of trust, knowing that the Father's love is greater than my faults and that I cannot lose it. Therefore I live Easter and I pass to the Father with Jesus, who takes me into his death to revive me with him.

You have to learn to depart, to leave. This sentence of Jesus leaving his disciples has a universal meaning: "It is better for you that I go." Besides, do we not die throughout our life? We are always taking leave of someone. We are constantly departing. These partial deaths occurring in our lifetime help us to consent to our last breath and to that of our loved ones. In the measure that we have learned to accept these partial deaths in our daily life, it will be easier for us to accept the departure of those who are dear to us, and to live our own dying as the last stage of growth in life.

Isabelle Delisle-Lapierre wrote well in her work, *Vivre son mourir:*

> If we have based all our existence on the search for money, the possession of many goods or the success of any task, it

> would be quite normal, when we see everything disappear, that we will be very tense, because if we have identified with our possessions, we will disappear with them.[106]

Entering Our Own Powerlessness

Old age and death are prepared for by gradually accepting *powerlessness.* Basically, the whole journey of Jesus through his temptations in the desert was the refusal of power. We can even, it seems to me, faithfully summarize the action and the message of Jesus by reducing them to a single issue: *power.* Let us reflect for a moment on the power of men over other men and on the various families of sin that it engenders: abuse of power directly, and the other forms, which are the abuse of knowledge or assets. Which of us, if he is completely honest with himself, can boast that he has never given in to the temptation of power, knowledge, or possession in his life? Notice for example, the temptation to be seen with people of authority who have power, to simply feel valorized in knowing a certain individual, minister, professional, or even a bishop, giving us the illusion that, by knowing them, we become greater and more important than we are. Henri Nouwen wrote:

> You all know what the third temptation of Jesus was. It was the temptation of power. "I will give you all the kingdoms of the world in their splendor," the demon said to Jesus. . .What makes the temptation of power so seemingly irresistible? Maybe it is that power offers an easy substitute for the hard task of love. It seems easier to be God than to love God, easier to control people than to love people, easier to own life than to love life.[107]

[106] Isabelle Delisle Lapierre, *Vivre son mourir: De la relation d'aide aux soins palliatifs* (Boucherville, Québec: Éditions de Montagne, 1987).

[107] Henri Nouwen, *Au nom de Jésus : réflexions sur le leadership chrétien* (Ottawa: Novalis, 1991); Henri Nouwen, In The Name of Jesus (Darton, Longman and Todd, 1989) [www.jkdoyle.com/the-temptation-to-be-powerful-henri-nouwen/ —Ed.]

Aging is to learn to let go, to choose love instead of control and to prefer the tenderness of intimacy to power.

It is surprising to realize that, for people in general, pride is less shameful than sexuality. It is even comparable with honor and good conscience but, nevertheless, it is pride and love of power that the Gospel calls into question more than anything. Whoever has power often places himself above others. Chapter six of Matthew's Gospel warns those who believe themselves to be righteous against the dangers that come to them from their good deeds: they risk simultaneously giving pretense to themselves as well to others. Whoever gives alms will be tempted to congratulate himself with his left hand about what he is doing with his right hand. The one who fasts must be wary of the peril of a reputation of asceticism that he is trying to portray to both himself and to others.[108]

Aging is accepting to enter into *powerlessness.* A human existence starts and ends by consenting to depend on God and men at the same time. To live evangelically, to accept aging and to prepare to die, is always an abandonment of power: either in a spirit of renunciation and simplicity in a "holy indifference," as mentioned by Saint Ignatius – which is not simply indifference, but peace of heart – or by leaving it to others when it is the age of handing over. From an *active* spirituality, we must move on to a *receptive* spirituality. The spiritual journey is to go from doing *[faire]* to letting go *[laisser faire]*, then allowing oneself to be *undone [se laisser faire]* and, in the end, to be *redone [se laisser refaire]* by God.

We may have tried in our past to *do* great things and we may have been tempted in our old age to continue to play the role we had in the past – with good will, certainly, and a real generosity, no doubt – the task of being efficient and useful to God and others. We must now move from generous good will to the spirit of faith and spiritual

[108] See more: "Avancer en âge" *La vie des communautés religieuses*, Nov-Dec-1989 (Montréal: RR.PP. Franciscains du Canada, 1992-2006).

childhood that will lead us to thanksgiving and to a contemplative sense of life. No one is indispensable but each one has a unique value. One day we must have the courage to tell ourselves and others the word Jesus announced of his departure to his disciples: "It is good for you that I go." Departing, leaving, letting go, abandoning: this is what we must learn as we age, because serenity and peace are at the end of this journey, from loss to loss, which leaves us, in the end, only our heart of a vulnerable child. How many persons dream, until the end of their life, of power and domination over their fellow human beings. Some old people, instead of abandoning themselves, even continue to exercise their power in a retirement center or in their families. They do not resign themselves to abandonment. Their whole life has been an attempt to be a little dictator and they end it by terrorizing their loved ones.

Giving Sense to Our Life

Every passing moment brings us closer to our death. All the transgressions or all the advances in the world cannot cure us of aging. Fighting against this aspect of life is pointless. We have to accept it. We have been aging since we were born. You age your whole life. And all of this life is a kind of capital which is nibbled away little by little from our birth until our death.

One day, a sociologist asked a sixteen-year-old girl: "What do you think of your old age." She answered: "I hope to die before it." It is probably quite normal at this age to say that.

We have to live every step of our life. It is necessary to be able to prepare the next step in the previous one. For example, the professional stage should be prepared for in adolescence, and the old age stage should be prepared for in middle-age and during the mid-life transition. Paradoxically, we see that those who are truly successful in their lives did not necessarily have to plan ahead, and those who are successful in their old age and death did not linger only in their preparation. They have lived by giving *meaning* to their life which continues in old age. They have learned to abandon themselves, to let go, and to truly love. True love is the best preparation for death.

To Reconcile with Our Finitude

Socrates said: "Our entire life must be a reflection on death and a training to face it." To face death, to be reconciled with the idea of our finitude and our mortality, is the condition, not only for reaching wisdom and serenity, but also simply for moving from infantilism to adult maturity. According to Miguel de Unamuno, "It is the discovery of death that gives peoples and individuals access to spiritual maturity." André Malraux confirms this: "The thought of death is the thought that makes man. We should celebrate the day when, for the first time, we have thought about death, because it is the day that marks the transition to maturity. Man was born when, for the first time, he murmured in front of a corpse: "why?"

In his book, *Pari sur la mort*, Vittorio Messori writes:

> Psychology and psychanalysis confirm the intuition of so many philosophers and writers, suggesting that human life can be divided into two periods: *before* and *after* the acceptance of our mortality. Whoever does not pass from the first phase to the second, adds these modern sciences, has no hope of becoming an adult.[109]

Of all that lives and dies on earth, we are the only ones who know that we are going to die. This is our misery, but it is also our greatness. Everyone no doubt knows Pascal's famous thought:

> Man is only a reed, the weakest in nature, but he is a thinking reed. There is no need for the whole universe to take up arms to crush him: a vapor, a drop of water is

[109] Vittorio Messori, *Pari sur la mort: L'espérance chrétienne: réalité ou illusion?* (Paris: Mame, 1984).

> enough to kill him. But even if the universe were to crush him, man would still be nobler than his slayer, because he knows that he is dying and the advantage that the universe has over him. The universe knows none of this.[110]

Why are we afraid to look at aging? Over the centuries, families and societies have always found a place within them for all ages of man. Children and young people were *hope*, adults were *maturity and strength*, old people were *experience and wisdom*. In the Bible, the elderly are protected by divine authority itself. "Stand up in the presence of the aged, show respect for the old, and fear your God. I am the Lord" (Lv 19:32). "Gray hair is a crown of glory" (Pr 16:31).

Today, we dye our white hair and hide our elderly so that they do not remind us too much of our own aging and the idea we do not want to face: that *we will die*. Basically, does the camouflage of old age not lead to the camouflage of death? This unconscious rejection of old age is only the premature rejection of our own aging. How many persons in their fifties or sixties never visit an elderly person in a retirement home or hospital? It is clear that these persons reject their own aging and the idea of their own death. We could even ask ourselves if the man of this end of the twentieth century would not be a man of all refusals: refusal of the unborn, refusal of changes to come, refusal to believe, refusal to evolve, refusal to suffer, refusal to age, refusal to die.

Our society refuses suffering and death; it hides death, it represses it, it does not want to face it. Society dreams that everyone will die without knowing it.

Christian Combaz wrote:

> In the meantime and for the time being, since death remains the end of the journey, it is above all necessary to disappear without being aware of it, so that, between active life and

[110] Blaise Pascal, A J Krailsheimer, *Collection les pensées* (London: Penguin Books, 1966); Blaise Pascal, A J Krailsheimer, *Pensees* (Harmondsworth: Penguin, 1986) [www.goodreads.com/quotes/394587 —Ed.]

> nothingness, there is nothing left. Do not succumb to the temptation to think; shrug off sickness and old age: in short, fatal immobility; die suddenly still fully active: this is the best way to end it. Heart attack, brain embolism, and the failed turn of a sports car are the only acceptable and dignified deaths.[111]

Above all, do not think: this is the new central theme of our "adolescent society." And Christian Combaz concludes with some sadness: "If we continue, I am not afraid to say, the West is inflicting on itself the dumbest old age in the world." Words undoubtedly too harsh, but which reveal the number of certain youth seeking in vain from the elderly a wisdom and serenity that is not found much anymore.

Confront the Idea of Death

"If we are unable to die," said the theologian Paul Tillich, "are we really able to live?"

Our adolescent society represses death and wants to deny suffering. We live a life where death is denied. Denial of death amounts to never allowing ourselves to face the anguish aroused by this last separation. Novelist Muriel Spark, in her book, *Momento Mori*, has one of the characters say: "If I had to start over, I would take up the habit of considering the idea of death. In this way, I would train myself, in a manner of speaking, to not forget about death. No other practice gives life such intensity. Without the sense of death, life is tasteless. You might as well eat the egg white and leave the yolk."[112]

Our society represses death, experiences of suffering and, above all, does not want to take the time to mourn the death of a loved one. Currently, some *crematoriums* offer families a facility like a funeral

[111] Christian Combaz, *Éloge de l'âge* (Paris: Robert Laffont, 1987).
[112] Muriel Spark, *Momento Mori* (Paris: R. Laffont, 1964); Muriel Spark, *Momento Mori* (London: McMillan, 1959).

fast-food restaurant that no longer makes death an event to mourn, and for taking the time to let our emotions live, but a news item to be forgotten as soon as possible. Therefore, at the death of a parent, a child, a partner, a brother or sister, the funeral business offers us its condolences by letting us, for a few hours and often less, be near the body of the deceased. Then, the family will request (paying fairly well) a priest or minister to celebrate a short liturgy before burning the body and inviting relatives and friends for coffee and the usual sandwiches. Funerals in the church, at least in big cities, decrease more and more because people prefer that all is done *quickly* and all in the same place. And that is not to mention those who, in their will, express the wish for their ashes to be spread in a lake or their garden. Truly, this gives pause for reflection on the *superficiality* of our modern Western society.

Cremation and Suicide

A book from Pierre Chaunu, a French historian, gave me pause for considerable reflection. One can be more or less in accord with his convictions, but it seems to me that one should have the honesty to first listen without prejudice.

In his volume, *Histoire et foi*, this is what he writes:

> Cremation aims to destroy not death but the fear of death. In our industrialized society, the multiplicity of crematoriums is an indisputable view of a fatal disease of the social body. The correlation is narrow between the advent of cremation and the collapse of fecundity and refusal of life. The scalpel on one hand destroys the "germ" in order to ensure non-progeny, and the effect at the other end of the chain destroys any trace of even an appearance of life, which could grow the odd germinations in cemeteries.[113]

[113] Pierre Chaunu, *Histoire et foi: Deux mille ans de plaidoyer pour la foi* (Paris: Éditions France-Empire, 1980).

He affirms that, "There is a correlation between cremation and suicide. Fear of death, refusal of life, cremation and suicide go together."

I do not know if a serious sociological study has been conducted on the fact that the suicides of young people between fifteen and twenty-five years old in the West, and even more in Quebec, began to increase appreciably when the *cremation* of the generation of their parents or grandparents became popular. I think that it would be interesting to study this more deeply. It is strange to think that in poor countries young people generally do not commit suicide and that cremation is almost non-existent among the Christians of these societies. Why then did cremation become so popular at the time of de-Christianization in Quebec? Is it only a coincidence? When we have lost the meaning of life and hope, death is suppressed and life loses its flavor. Learning to accept death is the secret to serenity and surrender. Oddly enough, most men and women today want to live a long life while, at the same time, they do not wish to get old. We would like to age and live a long time, while remaining young and beautiful and, above all, perform well from all points of view.

Death and Sexuality

Rollo May has an interesting remark about the thought of death being repressed in our present society: "The repression of death in our modern society leads to the obsession of sex...because sex becomes the easiest way to prove that you are still alive, to prove that you are still young, attractive and virile, to prove, in short, that you are not yet dead, and postpone the confrontation with your own death."

Looking at what is happening around us, we can only reflect on this idea reported by a sociologist: "A decadent society is a society which masks death and amuses the elderly."

To Accept Life

Before accepting death, however, one must have truly accepted life, and after having accepted life, one must accept to let go and accept the incomplete.

It is sometimes surprising to realize that it is the people who have accepted life, and who have not been afraid to give life and give of themselves, who die with serenity and even sometimes quite peacefully.

Elisabeth Kübler-Ross even goes so far as to say that the people who scream the loudest on their deathbed are *those who have never really lived.* They lived *superficially* and sometimes only *in their heads.* They have been life observers, not active participants. They were afraid of the risks. They secured themselves by their assets, but did not really live. Learning to age is the long journey to accepting being human, accepting to *choose life,* accepting to be moved and, after recovering our heart of a child, accepting to let go and to die.

Accepting the Incomplete

At the beginning of this volume, I spoke about accepting to be human and imperfect, but after the mid-life transition and when approaching old age, we must especially accept to leave, accept to depend, accept the unfinished.

In his volume, *Apprendre à vieillir,* Paul Tournier develops this theme and tells us that adults, until their fifties, are too often prisoners of their function and feel compelled to play a role, and then the mask falls little by little, and that is when they can come together and help children and young adults with their presence. As children, they do not claim to be self-sufficient. Young adults like to meet people who have accepted themselves and who radiate peace and serenity. This is why children and adolescents can often so easily come into contact with an elderly person. They are no longer afraid. It is then two hearts that meet and come together.

Paul Tournier says:

> To know the joy of aging, you have to be able to accept the incomplete. It is rare that a man can complete what he has set out to do. The incomplete always feels like failure. And when your children become adults, who among us can think of them with the good conscience of parents who have completed their mission? The pain of incompleteness is that of the human condition. Old age can be sweet for some, painful for others. But the suffering of the incomplete is universal, equal for all. Ever since childhood, consciously or not, man lives his finitude.[114]

Sooner or later, suddenly or gradually, every man discovers what philosophers call *his finitude*, that is to say, he cannot do everything, his prospects are limited. He becomes aware of his finiteness. As René Schaerer says: "Human reality is not: it is made, it is created... Incompletion is integral to my being. To live is to evolve ceaselessly, and it is to evolve toward death."

To accept the incomplete is to accept to leave and to die. Progressing towards death is not easy, but it is the path to serenity if it is accepted in peace.

Paul Tournier asks:

> What does it mean to accept? To accept is to say "yes" to life, but to the whole of life. When the child cannot detach from his mother's skirts, when he cannot assume his autonomy, he is already suspected of neurosis. When this adolescent cannot become an adult and take on adult responsibilities, he drifts into neurosis, because neurosis is always linked to an inability to progress. The adult who cannot accept

[114] Paul Tournier, *Apprendre à vieillir* (Paris: Delachaux et Niestlé, 1971); Paul Tournier, *Learning to Grow Old* (NY: Harper & Row, 1971).

> growing old, or the old person who cannot accept old age, or who accepts it reluctantly "because it is necessary," is experiencing the same difficulty, blocked in their evolution against the tide of life.

We prepare for old age and death by living wholeheartedly every stage of our life. Observe those old persons still brooding, who cannot accept their decline. There is, fundamentally, always a lack of acceptance and abandonment. Many of them have not come to terms with the active life they had before old age. They complained about their jobs and the responsibilities they had to take on; they regretted their childhood or their youth which, more often than not, they had not accepted either. The same yes must go through all of our life, which is successively a yes to a truly lived childhood, to adolescence, to youth, to adulthood, to old age and finally a yes to death. We turn the page of our existence more easily when we have filled it well. The Bible speaks of the patriarchs who died peacefully because they were "full of days" (cf. Gen 25:8).

Repression of Death

As I said earlier, our society is suffering from a new repression, no longer the repression of sexuality and its drives, but the repression of the idea of death and the denial of aging and mourning. The anguish of death does not disappear if one rejects the idea of death. Philippe Ariès said: "To forget death and the dead means doing a great disservice to life and the living." Carl Jung repeated: "A man who does not have a problem with death, and does not feel its tragedy, is in urgent need of treatment."

Fausto Gianfranceschi continues to deepen our reflection on current society and death by affirming:

> Formerly, the one who was about to die knew his condition: either because he understood the early signs, or because someone close to him had to warn him. Stronger than the

> fear of death was the fear of being deprived of one's own death, of not being able to participate in it with awareness and perfect disposition of mind. Now it is considered good practice to keep the truth from anyone with a fatal disease. It is said that this pattern has humanitarian intentions. But it is more of an inhuman rule, because dying without knowing it is to die twice.

When I was young, a prayer was recited which had been known in the Church for hundreds of years: "Deliver us, Lord, from sudden and unforeseen death," that is to say, one which hits us without our realizing it! Christians everywhere prayed to be spared from *sudden* death or during sleep, for this end was seen as a calamity for the whole man and not just for his *soul. To die without realizing it meant to be robbed of what is higher in human experience.* In the past, we prayed that we would *not* die suddenly or in our sleep, and today it is exactly the opposite. We do not want to suffer or face suffering and death, and we would like to die without realizing it. This is precisely the opposite of the ancient prayer of the Church. We dream of a sudden death, painlessly, and if possible, in our sleep. We do not want to approach death in a lucid manner by going through this last stage of our life. We do not want to live our death; we would like to deny it and erase it from our memory and our life.

In our society we must reconnect with the idea of death and relearn how to die.

Obsession with Health

Fear of facing death leads to obsession with sex and obsession with health at all costs. A doctor said with humor: "The obsession with health at all costs has reached phobic dimensions. The other day, a sixteen-year-old patient started crying in my office because in the morning her mother had not made her a Budwig cream.[115] It's

[115] Budwig cream is to facilitate a process of detoxification. ---Ed.

completely delusional. You don't take care of your soul anymore, you fear death, so you get your colon irrigated or call Doctor Albert."

Lise Langevin, president of the Agency for Public Health, concurred saying:

> Today, people have become obsessed with the body. If people want to be healthy, it is not even to feel better about themselves, it is only to be healthy. We have gone mad. Instead of walking around the block as before, we walk on a treadmill; instead of carrying boxes or climbing stairs, we lift dumbbells; and instead of doing a real bike ride, we go to the Nautilus Club and we climb on a bike that leads nowhere.

A psychologist, Jean Jacques Brochier, also placed the fear of death at the very basis of this obsession with health. "The current way of life of a whole generation testifies to the difficulties of our society with the idea of death, which tries to cover it up, to deny it by all means."

Currently, when people tell us about their retirement, they talk about it as if they would never get sick or die. They only want to make themselves secure with accumulated money and health that they want to keep at all costs. We even start having heart attacks from running to keep ourselves healthy or from doing too much social dancing. An eighty-year-old man collapsed at a Golden Age dance because he had been dancing nonstop all night. He probably wanted to prove to himself that he was still young and capable.

Learning to Leave

What do I know about death, except that I have to learn to approach it every day? I have to learn in everyday life to loosen the hold I often want to have on people, things, and events. I have to learn to die, to mourn, to slowly release my grip in order to open my hands and let go.

The greatest men, the most illustrious women, are dead, and one day I will have my date with death. I must already know how to let go. We believe ourselves to be so indispensable, and we look with pride upon the fruit of the labor of our hands and of all our works. A phrase from the Gospel should constantly dwell in our hearts: "We are unprofitable servants; we have done what we were obliged to do" (Lk 17:10).

Unfortunately, our projects often dominate us. They grab us. We know they can arise from our need to be recognized and admired. We often work out of so-called personal satisfaction to execute a project but, most of the time, we are driven by a desire for *performance and glory*. No doubt we work diligently and generously, but we are too attached to the esteem of others and to visible results.

In the face of aging and death, we must discover what is essential in life: *love* and *gratuity*. Sometimes, when the temptation comes to me to put my trust in everything I have done or accomplished in my life, I reread the text of this wise man from the Bible, Qoheleth:

> There is an appointed time for everything,...time to give birth, and a time to die; a time to plant, and a time to uproot the plant. A time to kill, and a time to heal; a time to tear down, and a time to build. A time to weep, and a time to laugh; a time to mourn, and a time to dance...A time to seek, and a time to lose; a time to keep, and a time to cast away... What profit have we from all the toil which we toil at under the sun? One generation departs and another generation comes...I have seen all things that are done under the sun, and behold, all is vanity and a chase after wind...But when I turned to all the works that my hands had wrought, and to the fruit of the toil for which I had toiled so much, see! all was vanity and a chase after wind. There is no profit under the sun (Eccl 3:1-6, 1:3-4, 1:14, 2:11).

The older we get, the more we have to discover the essential, that is *to be* and not *to do*. In the end, only *true love* and *the transparency of our heart* will remain. Everything else passes and will pass.

Aging As a Time of Purification

Old age can become a time of great purification. The loss of memory and dependence can be considered equivalent to the dark nights of Saint John of the Cross. In the night of the senses, first of all, everything is taken away from us: physical strength, health, sight, hearing, and the simple fact of moving, of dressing oneself. Everything is declining. But there is also the night of the mind: it is not uncommon for some elderly to experience great anxieties and to even sink into intense moments of depression.

In their volume, *De l'angoisse à la sainteté*, Brother Ephraïm and Doctor Mardon-Robinson write:

> For some, it will be humiliating to see themselves incontinent. They require much work, a very thankless job it must be recognized, so we do not always treat them with the gentleness and tenderness that they need. They encumber and they know it; they wait for death and, paradoxically, medicine strives to prolong them. Old age is the age of passivity; it is in this way that it is, properly speaking, contemplative. This last stage of life is, in terms of love, a second golden age, even deeper than infancy. The old person has nothing more to hope for in this world, which is why their anxieties can only lead to hope in God. There is no longer a place for self-will, love dominates everything; it is the age of the Holy Spirit. How many people, after having spent a whole lifetime away from God, will thus see themselves aspiring in their last years to be assimilated to the worker of the eleventh hour. But all this does not happen without struggle, without suffering, without agony. This is

> how old age can play the role of a purgative night in the full sense of the word, without counting the normal anxieties of death which are always present, even among the most excellent believers.[116]

The Time of Forgiveness

The approach of death is also the time of forgiveness with oneself, with others and with God. In my opinion, the elderly and the dying try to *reread their life*, to reconcile with their existence. They need to tell themselves and face to face with another person what they have experienced, bad and good.

In his work, *Ensemble face à la mort*, on accompanying the dying, Jean Vimont writes the following:

> I have met some sick people who, pressured by their remaining time to live, got going and carried out a kind of metamorphosis: they freed themselves from the money questions which had worried them so much by suddenly discovering that, in the face of death, these did not carry much weight; they were less worried about the future of their children, realizing that one direction or another, or that their children had so disappointed them, could finally be a good thing; everything became relative, secondary to the essential.[117]

We can change, even when death is near. Everything is recoverable. *The Good Thief* is an example. What appears from one end of the Gospel to the other is the primary importance of *conversion*, the reversal of being, which transforms one's gaze, becoming capable of considering all things in a different way. This conversion can change

[116] Mireille Mardon-Robinson, Ephraïm, frère de la communité des Béatitudes, *Le chemin des nuages ou la folie de Dieu: de l'angoisse à la sainteté* (Nouan-le-Fuzelier: Éd. du Lion de Juda, 1987).

[117] Jean Vimont, *Ensemble face à la mort: Accompagnement spirituel* (Paris: Le Centurion, 1987).

a whole life (*The Good Thief*), which seems easy for sinners who recognize themselves as such, and difficult, as we have seen, for those who believe themselves to be righteous: the Pharisees.

At the approach of death, we need to be *real.* One day an elderly lady visiting the dying walked into the room of a woman in her fifties who looked anguished and wanted to talk to someone. She humbly admitted to having lived a turbulent youth, typical of the end of the sixties and the beginning of the seventies, yet she had been raised in a very Christian family, but had let go of all moral and religious principles, and had not practiced her religion since her teenage years. Radiant, the good lady listened to her. The woman said to her, "How many children do you have?" The visiting lady replied, "Five children." – "Are you happy?" – "Yes." And after a long silence, through tears and sobs, she said: "I was too selfish; I always preferred myself. I have taken many trips; I have had a good time. I had only one child, but I could have had more. What do I have left now? I have missed my life."

The visitor then leaned toward the dying woman, taking her in her arms, and repeated this word to her from the first letter of Saint John: "If your heart condemns you, God is greater than your heart" (cf. 1 Jn 3:20).

This woman, on her deathbed, needed to reveal herself, she needed someone to tell her, by this welcome and this listening: "You are not totally these stupidities of which you speak...There is something more in you...the pure child in you is not dead. It can live again, even on the verge of death."

And this elderly lady, so good and so Christian, with delicacy and respect, persuades her to meet a priest. The dying woman remains alone with the priest for a good hour, confesses, receives Communion, attends Mass in her room, and is literally being transformed in a few hours: peace penetrates her, a kind of light illuminates her gaze. She asks for a rosary which she has not recited since her childhood, and dies almost transfigured by an interior light.

This is what a volunteer, full of tenderness and love, can do just by listening and welcoming with her heart.

Yes, old age and the approach of death are a time of forgiveness and reconciliation. It is never too late to change the way we look at our existence. And this is also true for guilt: it is never too late to cast away from us the evil we have done. But, for this, we must believe in infinite Mercy and must meet some persons transparent with the tenderness of God. All of this is necessary to face old age and death in a peaceful and serene manner. Let us not forget that the Prodigal Son of the Gospel succeeded in believing in his father's forgiveness and went "from death to life" (Lk 15:24).

To Uncover a Meaning to Our Life

Before their death, the elderly must remember their past with a kind of merciful tenderness. Far from being a sign of senility, as sometimes younger people may think, the elderly who look back on their past – their childhood, their youth, their middle years – are quite normal. They want to come to terms with their past and, with God's help, allow themselves to be forgiven, to forgive, and to forgive themselves. Like Joseph in the Old Testament, they can say to themselves that "everything has been permitted" for me to come to this point in my life. Everything could have been better, but this is who I have been and I throw the rest into the endless ocean of mercy. As Erikson puts it: "The integrity and wisdom of old age require looking at one's life with courage and mercy, and realizing that our life has meaning even though we have suffered and have not been that which we should have been." The elderly who have come to grips with their life, and made reconciliation with their past, recognize themselves in that they no longer shy away from solitude. They have become *welcoming* and *tender*, they love people without monopolizing them, they surrender themselves, they radiate a peace that often attracts the younger generation.

Dying in Peace

In the past, people died at home, surrounded by their children, and often the body was exposed in the house where the person had lived. Before leaving, we settled what we had to settle and some fathers or mothers asked to speak to each of their children alone. There was a special word for each, a particular message. We asked for forgiveness, often we reconciled, we asked for the priest, and we received Pardon and the Anointing of the Sick. We then entered our agony and the last fight with a certain peace, despite the natural anxieties of this last childbirth with the pain that is the preparation for eternal life. Death was not taboo. We fought against suffering, but we also accepted it with the Suffering Christ, in order to pass with Him from the Cross to Joy. We knew that there is no love without pain, that life is not easy, but that you have to enter this narrow path that leads to Life.

Without necessarily going back to a bygone past, could we not, without repeating all of our traditions, come back to take what is best? In this world which has lost the sense of true values, the new generation needs witnesses of love, people faithful to the end to true values, people who have not had it easy, but who have accepted the trials of life, who have made the renunciations necessary for their growth, and who die in peace at the end of their long journey of life leading to serenity.

Saint John of the Cross said: "At the end of our life, we will be judged on Love."

I Would Like to Say Goodbye

I would like to say goodbye to this fragile world
But goodbye tears me apart in violence to myself
And it is a hard battle between heart and soul
And it is a hard victory to die to yourself

In all the beating of this blood that burns me
Show me the freshness of the hurtful past
And the beauty of the world and the sap of the tree
Show me my common and beautiful seasons

My life is a waltz where summer abandons itself
My mouth will always have a trace of a wound
Like a taste of flowers, a taste of sour apples
Like yesterday's spring dreaming in my arms

I would like to say goodbye to this fragile world
Ah! Hold back my heart and do not sob
Because summer is sweeter when we already know
That death nestles on the blue edge of our eyelashes

To Recover Our Heart of a Child

To recover our heart of a child
We have to know how to leave things
Leave our dreams
Leave the roses
That perfumed all our springtime

To recover our heart of a child
We have to know how to cry over things
Cry for the losses
That life causes
Cry and laugh at the same time

To recover our heart of a child
We must know how to break things
These shells that we form
To protect our feelings

To recover our heart of a child
It is necessary above all to be ourselves
As we live
As we feel
Under our masks of cement

To recover our heart of a child
We must die very slowly
Die to ourselves
Die with time
Passing by and passing
By leaving

To recover our heart of a child
We must embrace our weakness
And kiss it tenderly
And forgiving our shortcomings
Open our arms gently
To what we are
Very simply

Verdun, a Summer morning in the month of August 1997

Death Can Come

Painfully unravelling my suffering
Life moves forward
As a leap of a wolf
At love's pace
Finally I manage to collapse
After so many years
In the deep ocean of childhood rediscovered

Everything happened so swiftly
O sweet wonder of living
I go on singing
Despite my heartbreaks
With this reality that inhabits me
That with each flower is pain enough

For the first time
I am reconciled with myself
And I regain my childlike heart
O impregnable joy
I finally know who I am
I open my arms to Love
That dwells within me

My God!

Death can come

. . .I am loved

Therefore I exist

Montreal, Summer 1997

The More I Advance My Heart...

The more I advance my heart and the more I discover you
Deep inside me in the recesses of memory
Beyond the years I discover
This masked child with such a sweet smile

I see him there with tears in my eyes
Resting in the bottom depths of memory astonished
As he is now and as he was before
When he awaited Easter at the end of a long Lent

Do you have to age a long time to become young
And finally not care about anything but him
This child so fragile in love with life
And who runs toward death in awe and trembling

How long does it take to accept life
With all its wounds and failures
And how many springtimes can we be assured
To see our cheeks wrinkled like a friend's

Five times ten years and it's fifty
And old age is approaching in silence
Embracing in its closed arms this child we have been
Whose life will pass as the mist in the sun

SELECTIVE BIBLIOGRAPHY

Adler, A. *Religion et psychologie individuelle comparée.* Paris: Payot, 1958.

Anatrella, Tony. *Non à la société dépressive.* Paris: Flammarion, 1975.

Artaud, Gerard. *Se connaître soi-même.* Montréal: Éditions de l'homme, 1978.

Assoun, P.-L. *Freud et le mystique.* Paris: "Nouvelle revue de psychanalyse," 1980. 22-39-67.

Baars, Conrad. *Born Only Once: the miracle of affirmation.* Chicago: Franciscan Herald Press, 1975.

Baars, Conrad, M. P. *Healing the Unaffirmed:* ***recognizing emotional deprivation disorder***. New York: Alba House, 1972.

Balmary, Marie. *Le sacrifice interdit: Freud et la Bible.* Paris: Grasset, 1986.

Buscaglia, Leo. *Apprendre à vivre et à aimer.* Montréal: Le Jour, 1983.

Combaz, Christian. *Éloge de l'âge.* Éditions Robert Laffont, 1987.

Daujat, J. *Psychologie contemporaine et pensée chrétienne.* Tournai: Desclée de Brouwer, 1962.

Dominian, Jack. *Maturité affective et vie chrétienne.* Paris: Éd. du Cerf, 1978.

Ferder, Fran. *Words Made Flesh: scripture, psychology and human communication.* Notre Dame, Indiana: Ave Maria Press, 1986.

Frankl, Viktor Emil. *Le Dieu inconscient.* Paris: Édition du Centurion, 1974.

Fromm, E. *L'art d'aimer.* Paris: Éditions de l'Épi, 1975.

Godin, A. *Psychologie des expériences religieuses.* Paris: Centurion, 1981.

Horney, Dr. Karen. *Neurosis and Human Growth.* New York: Norton, 1950.

Kelen, Jacqueline. *L'éternel masculin.* Paris: Robert Laffont, 1994.

Kelsey, Morton T. *Caring.* Paulist Press, 1981.

Macdonald, Gordon. *When Men Think Private Thoughts.* Thomas Nelson Publishers, 1997.

Maslow, A. *Vers une psychologie de l'être.* Paris: Fayard, 1972.

Messori, Vittorio. *Pari sur la mort.* Paris: Mame, 1984.

Parent, Michelle. *Expériences de Dieu.* Montréal: Éditions Paulines, 1983.

Payne, Leanne. *Crise de la masculinité.* Lausanne: Jeunesse en mission, 1985.

Sheehy, G. *Les passages de la vie.* Paris: Éditions Pierre Belfond, 1977.

Terruwe, Anne. *Amour et équilibré.* Paris: Apostolat des éditions, 1969.

Tillich, Paul. *Le courage d'être.* Tournai: Casterman, 1967.

Tournier, Paul. *Apprendre à vieillir.* Neuchâtel Paris: Delachaux et Niestlé, 1981.

Van Kaam, Adrian. *Religion et personnalité.* Mulhouse: Éditions Salvator, 1967.

Vergote, Antoine. *Dette et désir: deux axes chrétiens et la dérive pathologique.* Paris: Seuil, 1978.

Vergote, Antoine. *Psychologie religieuse.* Bruxelles: Charles Dessart, 1966.

APPENDIX

FAITH SHARING GUIDELINES

Recommended Guidelines

The "Decalogue for Faith Sharing" is recommended by the Families of Nazareth Movement USA for use with this book at small group meetings. It guides the participants in a group to share their personal reflections as a response to reading the text.

Recommended Prayer After Sharing

The prayer below is recited by an individual at the conclusion of their personal sharing. This becomes a signal to others that they may now share. It allows a person to express their thoughts completely without interruption.

Prayer After Sharing

Thank you, God, for allowing me to see the truth about my weaknesses and how it calls upon the abyss of your merciful love.

DECALOGUE FOR FAITH SHARING

1. **Meetings are led by the Holy Spirit.**
2. **The purpose of the meeting is:**
   - to become aware of my weaknesses and the truth of being loved by God.
   - to respond to the desire to deepen my faith.
   - to be open to others, my brothers and sisters in the group.
   - to share different experiences of my faith and how God is present in my life.
3. **When I go to the meeting, I will pray to God for others and myself.**
   - The prayer of empty hands or that of the tax collector is recommended.
4. **I will remember that I am God's child who has the right to trust and await miracles.**
5. **As a participant in our meeting I will:**
   - serve others and not count my own merits.
   - create the atmosphere of calm, focus/concentration and openness.
   - not impose on others my ways of thinking, reacting and perceiving.
   - avoid giving advice or solving others' problems.
   - speak from my personal "I" rather than use terms such as "you, we, us, people, we should, others do this."
   - avoid discussion and criticism.
6. **By keeping what is shared in the meeting confidential**, I will preserve each participant's freedom to share openly and protect their dignity as a child of God.
7. **I will not be afraid of moments of silence**, since I or somebody else may need time to reflect. Moments of silence provide us with unique opportunities for prayer and entrustment to God.
8. **I will remember to attentively listen** to what my brother or sister is saying in order to help them in the process of sharing.
9. **When I give a witness talk or share my faith, God's grace** is not only given to me but it is being multiplied and given to others.
10. **Above all, God expects from me humility and openness.** Even one person who is humble and open to God can create an appropriate climate during a given meeting that will spread to all participants. The most important and desirable goal is not the format of the meeting, but it is to be open to God's grace and presence.

Prayer After Sharing: ***Thank you, God, for allowing me to see the truth about my weaknesses and how it calls upon the abyss of your merciful love.***

OTHER BOOKS PUBLISHED BY IN THE ARMS OF MARY FUNDATION

THE WAY OF IMPERFECTION

by Father Andre Daigneault

In this book, Father Andre Daigneault explores the spirituality of the poor. The author asks his reader, "Can the poor, the injured of all kinds – the sinners with their wounds and through their falls – honestly aspire to holiness?" Holiness of the poor is to open oneself to merciful love: it is to discover that to love is not, first of all, being heroic, but it is to offer one's weakness, and to be open to God's gift in crying out to Him from the depth of one's poverty.

Fr. Daigneault explains that we do not build holiness through fidelity that can engender pride. In a heart poor and humble we receive holiness like that received by the Good Thief on the cross with the crucified Jesus.

Along with saints like St. Thérèse of the Child Jesus, Father Daigneault helps the reader discover this way of holiness – The Way of Imperfection.

THE GIFT OF FAITH

by Father Tadeusz Dajczer

An international bestseller in the field of Christian spirituality, this book about the interior life is a call to abandon oneself to God according to the Gospel edict: "unless you turn and become like children, you will not enter the kingdom of heaven" (Mt 18:3). With simplicity and clarity, the author manages to draw the reader's attention and awaken the yearning to experience God and to follow a specific path toward sanctity.

IN THE ARMS OF MARY

(a.k.a. PRAYING SELF- ABANDONMENT TO DIVINE LOVE)

by S. C. Biela

This book is the fruit of S. C. Biela's many years of deep reflections and insights regarding the Christian spiritual life. In it he explains and refers to the various stages of one's interior life and offers a pathway to deepening one's prayer. For this very reason, *In the Arms of Mary* can serve as a resource for spiritual renewal both for beginners and those who are more advanced on the path toward a "transforming union with Christ."

IN THE ARMS OF MARY FOUNDATION

P.O. Box 271987

Fort Collins, CO 80527-1987

If this book has helped you to appreciate God's immense love and mercy, please consider donating to **In the Arms of Mary Foundation**, a 501(c)(3) organization, to help spread this spirituality (Communion of Life with Christ through Mary) throughout the USA and the world. Send donation checks or money orders payable to **In the Arms of Mary Foundation** to the address above or donate directly on the website.

For more information about the **In the Arms of Mary Foundation** or to obtain additional books, holy cards, free downloads of *Reflections on Faith* topics, or to sign up for the Quote of the Day, please visit the website at **www.IntheArmsofMary.org**.

PRAYER CARD

Listen. Put it into your heart,
my smallest child,
that the thing that frightened you,
the thing that afflicted you is nothing:
Do not let it disturb you...
Am I not here, I who am your mother?
Are you not under my shadow
and protection?
Am I not the source of your joy?
Are you not in the hollow
of my mantle,
in the crossing of my arms?
Do you need something more?

Words of Our Lady of Guadalupe
Mother of the Americas
to St. Juan Diego, December, A.D. 1531

In the Arms of Mary Foundation
COMMUNION OF LIFE WITH CHRIST THROUGH MARY
www.InTheArmsofMary.org
1-800-451-1321

Holy cards can be obtain on
www.IntheArmsofMary.org

CPSIA information can be obtained
at www.ICGtesting.com
Printed in the USA
LVHW050205100123
736780LV00004B/396

9 781933 314679